THE FARMER,
THE COAL MERCHANT,
THE BAKER...

A PERSONAL IMPRESSION OF THE DEVELOPMENT
OF THE GELDERLAND HORSE WORLD

LIZ BARCLAY

YOUCAXTON PUBLICATIONS
OXFORD & SHREWSBURY

Copyright © Liz Barclay 2016

The Author asserts the moral right to
be identified as the author of this work.

ISBN 978-19111-7528-5
Printed and bound in Great Britain.
Published by YouCaxton Publications 2016

All rights reserved. No part of this publication may be reproduced, stored in a retrieval system, or transmitted in any form or by any means, electronic, mechanical, photocopying, recording or otherwise, without the prior permission of the publisher.

This book is sold subject to the condition that it shall not, by way of trade or otherwise, be lent, resold, hired out or otherwise circulated without the publisher's prior consent in any form of binding or cover other than that in which it is published and without a similar condition including this condition being imposed on the subsequent purchaser.

FOR ELZE

"A horse! A horse! My kingdom for a horse!"
From *The Tragedy of Richard the Third* by
William Shakespeare (1564-1616)

MAP DE ACHTERHOEK IN GELDERLAND

VALEGRO AND TOTILAS BREEDING LINES

```
                                              ULFT
                          FERRO
                                              BRENDA
              NEGRO
                                              VARIANT
                          FEWRIE
                                              MEWRI
VALEGRO
                                              VOLTAIRE
                          GERSHWIN
                                              APHRODITE
              MAIFLEUR
                                              HEIDELBERG
                          WEIDYFLEUR
                                              PETIT FLEUR
```

ULFT IS THE GREAT-GRANDFATHER of Valegro. The grandsire on the dam side of Ulft is Pericles. One of the great-grandsires of Variant is Amor. Both Pericles and Amor stood for the most part of their lives at stud 'De Radstake' with Johan Venderbosch in Varsseveld. On the dam side Voltaire is one of the grandsires. Voltaire was imported by Henk Nijhof and veterinarian Jan Greve from Germany.

Also Carl Hester's horse Uthopia, with the stallion Ulft on both the sire and the mare side, leads back to Pericles.

Four Year-old Totilas, Ridden by Jiska De Roos-van Den Akker, During the Pavo-Cup at Gorredijk. (Photo - Janneke de Rade)

				ENRICO CARUSO
			KOSTOLANY	
				KAPSTADT
		GRIBALDI		
				IBIKUS
			GONDOLA II	
				GLORIA VI
TOTILAS				
				NIMMERDOR
			GLENDALE	
				SILJA
		LOMINKA		
				AKTEUR
			ELSA	
				WOMINKA

Totilas is a prime example of the product of an open studbook. His sire Gribaldi is a Trakehner stallion accepted by the K.W.P.N. studbook.

The sire of Akteur is Amor, again this familiar name from the past.

§

Voltaire was an excellent show-jumper, having won Grand Prix's himself and this is what he generally passes on to his children. However, he is extraordinary in the fact that he produced some great dressage horses as well. Amor and Pericles were both crucial in the transformation from the Gelderland horse into the all-round competition horse and widely present in the breeding lines of the dressage horse of today!

PREFACE

When I left my farm in Cornwall on the way to Bristol airport, it suddenly struck me how much had actually happened, not only in my life, but in all the lives of the people I was on my way to visit. As Edward Bleekman more or less lived on the way to the airport, it seemed obvious to visit him before I would jump on the plane to Holland. For no real reason there are a fair few Dutch horsemen living in the south west of England and Edward Bleekman at Whorridge Stud near Cullompton is probably the most influential of all of them.

For years, before he moved to England in order to marry international event rider Clissy Strawn, he was an important part of stud 'De Radstake' owned by Johan Venderbosch, one of the people I was going to visit in the Netherlands. Hence the fact that an orientational chat with Edward would be a good start.

For some years now, I had been brooding about something. As a dressage trainer in the south west of England and also having trained some in the States, I had realized that the Dutch Warmblood had gradually become an international fact and phenomenon. From the professional Cornish jumping yard, owned and run by Claire Rushworth, to Terra Ceia, dressage yard owned by Donald and Jolande Williamson in Smithfield in the state of Virginia, yards that I instructed and trained in for many years, they all swore by the warmblood horse and they all knew the 'Gelderland horse', as they called it.

In 2009, sometime in August, I arrived in the yard of my first pupil in Cornwall who excitedly greeted me by saying: 'Liz, have you seen…?' She could not stop talking about this unreal horse with its amazing rider. It was of course Totilas with Edward Gal at the European Championships with a score of 90.70% for the Freestyle, a world record. That day, whichever yard I entered, it was the first thing every single person talked about.

Later, when this so-very-special relationship ended in such a sad and bizarre way, I watched them together on YouTube at the stallion show in 2010 and it was impossible to keep my eyes dry when watching this wonderful horse rise to the occasion and never let the ecstatic audience down, with yet more piaffe, more passage, more flying changes, as the crowd kept the rhythm going with their hands and feet.

And then came Valegro with Charlotte Dujardin ... more talk, more excitement, this time because the English had done it! With Charlotte and Valegro having been instrumental in making it happen. Team Gold at the London Olympics in 2012 and a fantastic individual Gold for Charlotte and Dutch-bred Valegro. Carl Hester's horse Uthopia, again a Dutch product, came in with a grand fifth.

And slowly it started to dawn on me that in Gelderland I knew some of the people who had made this happen, who had actually been crucial to this development. And they were getting older, and they had a story, and I wanted for them to tell that story because I knew it was special.

So this is where the story starts. I contacted four horsemen from Gelderland. All four had at some point stuck in my memory for various reasons. Some were breeders, others trainers or instructors and they had all competed at some point in their lives. All these men knew each other and often their lives intertwined - the horse world is a small world anywhere in the world.

Once all had committed themselves to meeting me, I booked my trip, excited about what might come of it.

On arrival in Holland, I planned all my visits and after a few days of preparation and catching up with my sister and some friends I started driving around the area where my roots lay, the province of Gelderland, the home of the Gelderland horse. I was welcomed everywhere I went. Stud owner Henk Nijhof from 'Team Nijhof', breeder Johan Venderbosch from 'De Radstake', event rider and trainer Jan Oortveld, instructor and former coach of the international eventing team Roeli Bril, they all gave me plenty of time and were very patient with me. As a matter of fact, I think the reminiscing was something they all loved doing and I knew from my research that this was not the first time they had told these stories.

§

The excitement began each day, as soon as I would leave my sister's apartment in the *Hanzestad* Zutphen, a small and very charming town bordering the river IJssel. The walk to the car through the small brick-laid streets with the narrow high façades of the town houses on either side, some of them elaborately decorated along the edge of their short but steep roofs, hiding their red tiles, others smartly embellished above their windows. Then I would drive, first along the river IJssel, curving proudly through the fields, transporting water that had travelled all the way from Austria, Switzerland and Germany.

Driving along the dyke, through the beautiful farmland, I would feel my chest widen, greedily taking in the space of this flat land with its horizons so very far away in all directions. The fields were often bordered by a stream or ditch with, along it, typical Dutch ancient knot willows, occasionally interspersed with woodland, where the forever-straight lanes were flanked by long, proud rows of tall beech trees. The windmills, the thatched roofs of the old farmhouses and their colourful wooden shutters, all often relating to the estate they belonged to.

I had loved growing up in the countryside in Gelderland and, still, my best friends are from there. It was idyllic for a youngster to grow up with such freedom, wandering around the lanes on my pony, visiting a friend's farm, staying there for the weekend or even an entire holiday.

§

In the next few weeks, on these wonderful and often melancholic trips, speaking to some of the most knowledgeable Dutch horsemen anywhere, I was reassured that I was correct in thinking that my childhood Gelderland had been the hub of the conversion of the Dutch Warmblood from workhorse to the modern sport horse it has become. This process had started well before the Second World War, but first took a huge flight in the sixties and seventies of the previous century. In my childhood I had watched this happen and only now did I realize the enormous impact of that process on the entire equestrian world. Not only do the top Dutch riders compete on their Dutch-bred horses but the rest of the world does too and, at the time of writing this book, Charlotte Dujardin is of course the first name that comes to mind.

§

Initially most breeders were farmers and they produced their own offspring from foal to ridden horse as well as they could. This was a multi-purpose horse, used just as much for dressage as for jumping - or driving of course, and they were also still used to do some farm work. As the breeding world became more professional and some of those farmers converted to breeding horses for a living, they found that they either had too many horses to ride themselves or realized that they simply needed the skill of the professional riders to do the job for them. This triggered a whole new era, an era which is still with us to this day. Many professional riders compete stallions for the big studs these days. In 2012 the Dutch newspaper *Trouw* wrote that Holland is now the fourth biggest exporter of sport horses in the world with a turn-over of 159 million euros. Somewhere between 6,000 and 8,000 horses are leaving the country every year, the number still growing.

§

Blood is thicker than water and that is exactly what drives the horseman. There is no escaping the power of the desire to succeed, either in breeding or producing stallions to breed with, to train these powerful and elegant animals or to train the riders who want to become their trainers; it is a way of life that is all-encompassing and demands never-ending commitment.

So here is a little bit of history, a personal impression of the Gelderland horse world, four stories of horsemen who were born just before, or during or just after the Second World War. Each in his own way has put his stamp on the development of the Dutch horse business, which today knows no borders. All were born and bred in the province of Gelderland in the east of the Netherlands, and all, somewhere in my youth, touched my life in some way or another. Often, at various times, whether it was when I bred some horses myself or during the training of many of them, I think of them and of what they taught me, directly or indirectly.

This is not a technical essay about breeding or training; that is already widely available in the many equine magazines and on the studbook websites. This is about a way of life, a way of life that has quietly slipped away and is all but gone - although fortunately still available from the mouths of the men who lived it.

I want young and aspiring owners of Dutch Warmbloods anywhere in the world to understand and appreciate the story of how it all happened and the blood, sweat and tears lost on the way by these hard-working people. When looking at their KWPN papers, the chances are that owners of Dutch Warmbloods will recognize names of some of the legendary stallions in the stories in this book as possibly the great- or great-great-grandfathers of their own beloved steeds. Stallions who were bred, produced and ridden by these Gelderland horsemen.

WORD OF THANKS

I would like to thank Henk Nijhof, Johan Venderbosch, Edward Bleekman, Jan en Gon Oortveld and Roeli and Toos Bril for their time and patience. It was an enormous joy to be given the chance to search the past together, reminisce and roam through the endless stacks of pictures, sometimes having to be dug out from the attic in a suitcase!

Thank you Bob, for keeping me out of trouble, I learned a lot!

DWR, without the opportunity you gave me, no matter how short-lived, this possibly would not have happened. Also, you made the effort to keep me factually correct.

Maarten, the interest you showed and to make the contact with Jiska was invaluable to me.

Jiska, thank you for helping without even knowing me.

Thank you Henk, Lies and Ronald for your help and support. Your patience to read with me gave me the confidence to finish what I started.

Thank you Mir, for sharing some of the emotional turmoil.

And of course Buz, sorry you had to listen to it all, over... and over... and over...... again.

Contents

Valegro and Totilas Breeding Lines — xi
Preface — xv
Word of Thanks — xxi

Growing Up in Gelderland — 1
KWPN History in a Nutshell — 23
Stud, Breeder and Trainer; Each Can't Live Without the Others — 27
Johan Venderbosch — 31
Henk Nijhof — 51
Jan Oortveld — 67
Roeli Bril — 77
A Visit to the National Stallion Show 2016 in Den Bosch — 91

Afterword — 99
Explanations and Translations — 101
Sources — 102

1

GROWING UP IN GELDERLAND

Somewhere in the old trunk my grandmother left me, a photograph has been mischievously hiding itself for over twenty years now. It was taken in 1962 and happens to be my favourite picture of my dad and me and every so often, its skill at hiding being so great, yet another frantic search ends in frustration. The scenery in the photo is one of those rectangular and seemingly floating fields surrounded by narrow ditches filled to the brim with what my country has most of - water. My dad, in suit and tie, because that is how one went to visit friends or family in those days, is holding a huge, dark, bay mare who is quietly grazing. On top is me in a cute little, light-blue frock and frilly socks with tiny white sandals, three years old and beaming from ear to ear.

The photo was taken at the farm of my eccentric uncle, a rather untidy dairy farmer who married my dad's older sister. Our family would visit once a year, because we lived in the east and they in the west of the country and first our white Volkswagen Beatle, later our little grey Vauxhall Viva did not move so very fast.

I cannot remember much from those visits other than that the milk used to be collected by an official vehicle which resembled something like an ambulance.

Because the farm was near Amsterdam, we used to visit my grandmother on the same day. She had the cosiest apartment in a five-story-high apartment building, built just after the Second World War and typical for that part of Amsterdam. Although she had lost most of her family money to my drunk of a grandfather, she had somehow managed to hang onto some very old and beautiful furniture and several imposing oil paintings, and this despite their fiery divorce. I loved to sit on the soft cream-coloured carpet facing the bookcase with a cup of hot chocolate and leaf through the ape section of her black, leather-bound encyclopaedia, all the while with one ear open to the conversation between my parents and my grandmother. These conversations indeed gave me some extraordinary information: the dairy herd of my uncle was found to have T.B.; the milk was collected by the official vehicle in order for it to be destroyed. My uncle was given a fair sum of money as a recompense. This had been going on for years. My uncle was very tight with his money and tough on my aunt so she never had any money for herself. She solved this by letting her Siamese female cat go astray and come home pregnant. She sold the kittens as 'half bred Siamese' for good money (which she hid) to many innocent Siamese-cat lovers.

On the way back home I probably dreamed of sitting on that great big horse again. The horse which, other than doing all the work the tractor did in later years, probably also had a foal every year which would be sold off until eventually one would be kept as a replacement for when its mum had grown too old to do all the hard labour.

§

My dad had a chequered childhood. After a dirty divorce from the mother of his children, my drunk of a grandfather married another beautiful wealthy lady and my grandmother had no option other than to escape to Amsterdam and clean the houses of people she would have gone to have tea with before her life changed so dramatically. Reduced to poverty, she was not in a position to care for her two youngest: my dad and his younger sister. My dad was left to live in Zwolle with one of his schoolteachers when he was sixteen years old, having to leave the impressive, white-plastered townhouse along the IJssel in Kampen, where my grandfather continued his dental practice between his drinking spells.

§

It is too long ago to recall the exact time frame, but it was probably about five or six years after our last trip to visit my grandmother and, this time, the only picture is just one in my head. My dad and I were on a (for him) melancholic trip, following the path of his childhood. We were driving along the river IJssel between the '*Hanzesteden*', the towns Zwolle and Kampen. My dad had taken me on this drive on a beautiful and sunny spring day along the fast-flowing river with its barges laden with sand or stone, deep in the water or empty with most of their black hulls above, proudly flying the tricolored Dutch flag on their stern and going fast when pushed by the fast-flowing mass of water or struggling against it when travelling the other way.

We were driving to the farm where my dad used to go on his bike, during the war when he was just fourteen years old, in order to collect butter and maybe some eggs. Some of the roads were often under water back then because the IJssel would flood large stretches of land during late winter or early spring. Also, all bikes were confiscated by the Germans and people used to remove the tires so as to make them useless. This resulted into my dad's five-kilometre trip, or the most part of it, being through foot-deep water on a bike without tires. One day he came home only to realize that somewhere along the trip the butter had dropped from the back of his bike. He was made to go back and look for it, of course without any result. It makes me weep when I write this down.

Having arrived at the farm we were greeted with such warmth. There were the parents whom my father had visited back then, now older and living in a separate part of the farmhouse. The son who had taken on the farm and who was a similar age to my dad, remembered him very well. He introduced his wife and everybody shook hands. Their two adolescent sons came in because they were keen to see who the guests were. The wife poured coffee and I was given a glass of lemonade. The banter was loud and cheerful despite the fact that they knew each other from desperate times. Not only had this family helped many to food whenever possible, they also had hidden Jewish people during the war.

It was a big farm, now once again prosperous and wealthy, so there were quite a few workhorses and some youngsters. The farmer told my dad proudly that he was in the process of buying a tractor. When my dad and I went outside to be shown around, one of the sons happened to come around the corner of the old, thatched, Flemish brick barn with two dark brown, nearly black, youngsters. They were big and stalwart, full of life, dancing on their halters with the grinning young lad very relaxed between them, confident those two teenagers were not going to hurt him.

I was in awe, completely overwhelmed by this stunning sight, and later that evening, lying in my bed I fought sleep in order to not lose the picture, still so very clear in the darkness of my small bedroom, of those two beautiful horses playfully bouncing on their halters and in their midst the healthy young farmer's son.

§

Every year, sometime in early spring, during the first dry spell when winter knew it had to give way, the farmer who owned the field opposite our newly-built house on the very edge of the village of Brummen would appear with his two strong horses in front of the plough. Although some forty-five years ago, I can still hear, see and smell the grunting, the sweat and the turning of the huge clumps of river clay. The horses making the sharp turn just outside our front door, the inside horse having to hold back while the outside horse had to work hard to keep up. Farmers were still strong and fit men in those days.

§

Occasionally I would hop on my bike and visit farmer Koppel Gerritsen on his farm not more than half a mile from where I lived. At that time, he was the competent and much loved instructor for the riding club 'de IJsselruiters' but that was not of any interest to an eight-year-old horsey girl. What mattered was that he wore clogs and I loved clogs, and he had a Landrover with his Dalmatians in the open back in which I was allowed to join them for a drive through the fields in order to check on the broodmares and youngsters.

One dark winter evening, my dad and I visited together. We walked through the yard covered in slushy snow, left over from a cold snap, and entered into the old barn through the bottom half of the large, dark-green barn door. Both sides of the wide, concreted area in the middle were lined with dairy cows, which had just been milked, their chains rattling every time their heads moved slowly up and down as they patiently chewed their hay from the troughs, their body heat creating a warm and humid environment. My dad went to talk to Koppel and I went to sit on a huge heap of sugar beets at the end of the barn, not at all bothered about their lengthy banter because I loved watching and listening to the relaxed munching sound of the hay between the rotating jaws of the cows. It always made me feel at ease to be among the dairy cows and I would pretend to be living there on the farm, to be part of it.

My dad and Koppel made some joke and I felt that their grin was directed towards me. I believed it involved the young boy who was helping and although I did not quite understand, it did make me blush.

§

A little further on from Koppel was a modern-built house with stables and an indoor school. The fields around were fenced beautifully and the entrance gate was particularly impressive. I knew who lived there; Tjeerd Velstra his name was and he was a show-jumper. Many an afternoon after school I spent there, waiting in hope that the gates would open and someone would notice the little girl in her red rubber boots and invite me in. Of course that never happened. From where I was stood, I could only see the horses in the distance, beautiful horses, being led in and out of their fields, or, tacked up, disappearing into the indoor school.

§

Pony club 'De Viersprong' with Mr. Pasman as our instructor in 1973.

When I was twelve we moved to the other side of the IJssel to a small farmhouse not far from the tiny village of Toldijk. By now I finally had my own pony, a Haflinger bred by my wealthy godfather and sold to my dad for tuppence. One day my dad and I visited the chairman of the local pony club 'De Viersprong', a man by the name of Willem Breukink. He was a huge man with a loud voice, a rather red face and short-cropped white hair, handsome in his own way. He ran a reasonable size dairy farm on the edge of our village and had donated a little piece of land for the pony club to have a meeting place in order for the children to have their weekly training.

OOM WILLEM AND TANTE GERRIE WORKING
THE LAND WITH THEIR HORSES.

My dad had brought me to yet another cosy farmhouse kitchen with the coal stove at the centre and the perpetual coffee pot on top. *Oom* Willem and *tante* Gerrie, as I would soon be calling them, had two sons and a daughter who was a few years younger than me and a proper tomboy. As a matter of fact, I was a little scared of her. That first time we were sitting in their kitchen, my dad comfortably chatting away with the man who was to become a very good friend, this girl got up, walked slowly towards me and just stood staring at me until her mother told her off. The blood was pounding in my head and I felt vulnerable. She properly scared me, and when she asked me to go outside to play, I wasn't that keen. Soon, though, we climbed up into the rafters of the barn where the hay was stacked high above the cows, then moved on to the calf shed and stuffed our faces with dried calves milk to prove to each other we were not shy of anything. A friendship for life was cemented that day.

Later in the year this family moved to another farm in the same area, possibly the biggest around, but right close to the IJssel river near the village of Steenderen. It became my second home. I adored my friend's dad who nicknamed me 'Jenne', Jenne being a very old-fashioned girl's name from the country, and I treasure that name to this day.

§

My friend and I spent endless hours galloping through the fields along the river, smoking our first cigarettes, having hidden ourselves behind the dyke, basking in the sunshine or lying low to avoid the rain and wind, trying to smother our mischief and dreaming together about who we each were going to date one day.

When it was time to move on from a pony to a horse, my friend's dad bought a KWPN mare for her who was also bred every year. Once a year the lorry with the stallions from Venderbosch drove up with Edward Bleekman behind the wheel. The mare was hobbled and covered if she was showing that she was ready, 'blinking' it was called. Afterwards the stallion hopped back on the lorry as quickly as he had come off and Edward would only turn up again if the mare 'returned', meaning the sperm hadn't taken.

The lorry had a side ramp with two or three stallions on it so the mare owners could choose which one they wanted without too much hassle unloading. These stallions lived for the whole covering season on this lorry from early morning until well in the evening, travelling around from one love affair to the next. There were still many years to come before artificial insemination was common practice and would change this.

So, us kids, we all saw many great stallions, who are now the backbone of our studbook, dance off and on the lorry in order to do their job and this in our own backyard. Little did we know that we were watching an international project unfold!

§

It was normal to work a mare as close as possible to her giving birth. She would only have a few weeks off before foaling and soon after foaling the training and competing would start again. When going to shows the very young foals would travel with the mare in the trailer and have a drink between classes. Once they were slightly older they would simply be left at home in the stable. Farmers were very matter of fact about that; the animals were there to serve them, just as when they were still working the land. It certainly culled out the ones who couldn't cope - and in those days horse meat was still eaten by most and a common sight in the butcher's shop. It was often on our table as a smoked luncheon meat. I ate it quite happily until my friend's pony had to be put down because of laminitis. It just wouldn't go down my throat after that.

§

Just as my friends, I was moved up from pony to horse. Mine was a 15 hand cross between a New Forest pony and Flying Sandy, an Anglo-Arab belonging to a one-legged man. This one-legged man led his own stallion off and on the lorry for the mare visits. How trusting their relationship was.

When I turned up at the riding club for lessons with my 15 hander, the fathers of my friends shook their heads in disapproval; for a farmer, anything under sixteen hands was a waste of time.

§

That time was a great time, when farmers were sowing the seed for what was to become the modern Dutch Warmblood, a time of unassuming fun and excitement. It was the beginning of the development of the grading shows and riding club competitions, always on grass and sometimes in mud. Everybody taking part in both show-jumping and dressage, some excelling in one or the other with their fellow riding club members and friends cheering them on or making rude jokes about their riding ability.

For me both the highlight, but also the saddest moment, of my time with the riding club came when I was seventeen and my dad was still chairman of the local pony club 'De Viersprong'. I won the trophy my dad had donated for the highest placed local rider at our riding club area competition. My dad was not able to be there anymore because he was in the hospital, very ill and dying. My round of honour was fast and blurred with tears; my little horse, which had helped me to win, was unstoppable and so we went around twice actually. After that, when some two hundred competitors left the arena, four in each row, sitting trot, stirrups clanging together, I saw my dad's great farmer friend, *oom* Willem, a few tears running down his big red cheeks, yelling, 'well done, well done, Jenne!!'

Still next to my bed: the little Viersprong Cup my dad donated as chairman of the Pony Club.

§

Sometimes a gang of us would meet up. I was the only one who was not from a proper working farm but this didn't deter me from feeling like one of them. We would wander through the fields from one farm to another and look at the youngsters, sometimes ten or more in a field, make them run and point out to each other which we thought was the best mover, the most expressive or whatever else we could think up. These youngsters were two or three or more generations down from the Gelderlander farm workhorse. The fathers of my friends had increasingly started to use thoroughbred stallions from studs such as Venderbosch in Varsseveld and Henk Nijhof in Geesteren, two farmers who had dared to go ahead and invest in these thoroughbred stallions, something the regional studbooks were not quite ready to support. This investment in thoroughbred stock was a breakthrough and catapulted to another level the process of breeding a more versatile, finer and more agile horse. These horses were far more exciting to ride and show up with at the local riding clubs, clubs the farmers had started, and the standard of the riding clubs and the level of performance at shows increased accordingly.

Each club had its own local instructor and everyone would meet, probably on a Saturday, for a group lesson. When I joined the local riding club our instructor was a local farmer with a great love for and knowledge of horses, who still used to long rein his young horses in the arena, a technique that was gradually replaced with lunging for horses that were ridden rather than driven. I loved watching *oom* Hans Vleemingh because he always looked so calm and controlled, the way he did it, his quiet, low voice making the horse at ease. It was an art that added a whole other dimension to controlling a horse's balance.

A VERY YOUNG OOM HANS VLEEMINGH ON HORSEBACK.

It was *oom* Hans Vleemingh who, when still a young boy, had begged his father to have Gelderland draught horses rather than the very heavy Belgian horses. He wanted to ride so badly that his endless pleading persuaded his father into selling the Belgians and buying some Gelderland mares, despite concerns that they would not be as suitable for the work on the farm. On arrival, the first job these Gelderland mares had to do was pull the carts with freshly harvested sugar beets out of a wet field in wintertime, one of the heaviest jobs, tougher than ploughing because that could only be done when the ground had dried up sufficiently. When the sugar beets were ready the ground was nearly always sodden and the horses had to come up with every bit of strength they possessed in order to bring the heavy-laden cart back to the farm.

THE GELDERLAND MARES WORKING THE LAND.

The farm worker came home so very excited. 'They tip-toed through the mud effortlessly, barely touched it!!' The father was as pleased as the young son, who could now start his riding career. As the years went by he used his father's farm to breed many a good horse. When married to his wife Evelien, they would consider it a Sunday outing to visit farms together where young foals had just been born. He would 'sketch' them, meaning, he would note all their markings on a piece of paper, which would be used by the studbook in order to prepare the papers to go with the newly born. This is how this couple often spent their spare time together, *oom* Hans sketching, *tante* Evelien maybe reading or doing a little sewing that she possibly had taken with her.

For this *oom* Hans was rewarded with the Silver Pin by the KWPN.

But Saturdays were devoted to the local riding club and whenever there was any other opportunity to pass on his riding skills, he did so with all the patience in the world.

THE KWPN SILVER PIN FROM OOM HANS VLEEMINGH.

§

With two other friends we were waiting for the small ferry to bring us to the other side of the IJssel river. It was freezing cold and the snow was like dust and plenty of it. We were on our way to the small farm of Hendrik Jan Wassink, a bachelor in his fifties who to us younguns seemed ancient. He had several horses and, although on most farms the tractor had replaced horsepower, he still worked his land with his horses, as that was how he liked it. Hendrik Jan always smiled, was always happy to give anybody who turned up on his doorstep a good time.

ON THE SLEIGH WITH HENDRIK JAN WASSINK HOLDING THE ROPE REINS.

We did not have to twist his arm very hard for him to put two grey mares in the harness in front of the beautiful sleigh. Soon we were sliding fast and smooth through the crispest snow, with, on one side, the river and on the other the dyke and in between the quiet land, only disturbed by the sound of the horse's feet and laughter... oh, what a wonderful way to be young!

TWO YOUNGSTERS IN THE SNOWY LANDSCAPE ARE WATCHING US AS THE SLEIGH PASSES THEM BY.

§

Hendrik-Jan had lived on this farm his whole life and his father before him. The farm was part of the Reuversweerd Estate. We used to play near the huge and ghostly house which had lost its grandeur in the saddest way thinkable. During the war Baron von Sytzama had been taken by the Germans and, together with seven others, he was shot. His wife, the baroness, left the house immediately and ruled that it should never be lived in again. The clock at the front of the house stopped at twenty-past-two with no one left to rewind it.

Towards the end of the war Hendrik-Jan and his family had to leave their farm because they were in the middle of crossfire. They watched from a distance and helplessly saw their farm burn down and their young bullocks go wild for fear in the field. Thirteen of them died from bullet wounds.

Soon the war was over and the chaotic bewilderment of freedom set in. It was only some two weeks later that they were able to bury the decaying bullocks which were giving off a terrible stench. To do the job they had a special crew. NSB-ers, their heads shaved for shame, were Dutchmen who had sided with the Germans; they were given shovels and told to get on with it.

§

On a sunny day we drove off to Deurne, the impressive Dutch equine college, based on the system the Germans developed in order to produce their trainers and instructors. The local doctor and horse-lover, Wiegersma, had designed a beautiful cross-country course, a novelty in those days because there were not that many around. I was very excited because this was the day of my interview with Mr. Tjeerd Velstra, the same man who owned the modern yard in Brummen where I once used to stand outside the big iron gates. He was now director of Deurne and was known to be a strict and powerful man. Local riding club instructor *oom* Hans was driving, his wife *tante* Evelien sat next to him and my mum and I sat in the back.

On arrival we were shown around and I very vividly remember the sawn-off legs of slaughtered horses lined up per four in a row in the biology classroom. I had been forewarned by other students and I was not wimpish about things like that anyway. However, two hind legs and two front legs, cut off halfway up the cannon bone and with the solid black, shiny, enormous feathers obviously belonging to a Friesian horse stuck with me. The white bone and the fresh blood on the edges, where skin somehow became meat, shone bright and in my imagination I could hear the shoes clanging on the tarmac as these legs still proudly moved in a brisk trot along a small Dutch road in front of a smart carriage.

My interview with Mr. Veldstra was nerve-wrecking. All I can remember is that at the end he said with a grin that I would probably do well, provided I kept my little nose down.

If I remember correctly, the system was that you worked as a learning pupil at a recognized yard for nine months of the year and the other three months you were in Deurne for a very intense time of tuition. I learned a huge amount in the eight months at 'De Liemers', a yard on the border with Germany. I passed my exam in order to be allowed into my first year at Deurne. Boss Thea Oortveld taught me to drive a carriage and I passed an exam for this. I sat on my first green and unbacked horse with her brother Jan Oortveld, grinning mischievously, holding the lunge line and in charge of my well-being. I fell off jumping, got stuck with my foot in the stirrup and was dragged around the riding area the day my mum happened to be there and somehow I managed to convince her to not take me home. I was left to my own devices with a green and naughty pony, lost my temper, overstepped the mark without anybody seeing it and cried, with my head buried in her mane, for her to forgive me. I started to give my first lessons. I also learned to drink, get drunk - and not do that again.

It wasn't to be, not yet anyway, life had other things in store. I left the yard the day the diggers arrived in order to double the size of the existing indoor arena and was replaced by someone who passed every exam with flying colours. The reason I know this is because, just like me, he also moved to the south west of England where, many years later, we ended up competing against each other.

ON MY WAY TO PASS MY DRIVING TEST.

§

After a hefty collision with a car when riding my moped, it took several years to get back in the saddle, but in my mid-twenties I was finally able to take up training again. I loved riding for Ingrid and Theo van Dijk at 'Stal de Eik' in Holten, a beautiful area near a lovely stretch of gently sloping moorland. These people were true horse-lovers, consciously choosing to be small-scale in order for all the horses to be able to have sufficient 'field time'.

Ingrid was extremely strict in her training and demanded that no horse was ever trotted or cantered before at least ten minutes' walk and also that every training session was finished in the same manner. No matter how kind Ingrid was, if she caught you breaking this rule she would be livid. This stuck with me forever and I've passed it on to my pupils ever since.

Every two weeks instructor Roeli Bril would turn up for a lesson with Ingrid's daughter Sandra. For half of that lesson I could bring in one of the horses and share with her. Roeli was well known for his expertise and I've always been grateful for the opportunity to learn from him. Roeli was the nephew of a coal merchant in Zutphen and by the time I met him he was already an authority in the horse world, training and competing at the highest level in both show-jumping and dressage. And it did not stop there. We met again years later at Burgley in England. By then Roeli was the coach for the Dutch eventing team.

§

Some twenty years ago I trained in the States for some years, at a small but very professional yard in Smithfield, an area in the state of Virginia. Donald and Jolande Williamson had bought some warmblood broodmares which had produced several offspring. Also, Jolande had a dressage horse which she competed at Prix St. Georges level and a very promising four-year-old chestnut gelding. Donald and Jolande took me to some warmblood auctions near Charlottesville in the Blue Ridge mountains. I did not like the horse auctions. It distressed me to see horses, especially the innocent youngsters and foals being chased around by a bunch of yelling over-excited men accompanied by the loud auctioneer taking the bids in an equally over-excited manner. The thought that these horses had no power over their own lives hit me with every crack of the auctioneer's hammer. They looked so desperately lost and lonely, not understanding one bit about what was happening to them.

Donald had a phenomenal eye for a sensible horse. He knew he was buying for the hobby rider who would not be able to deal with a headstrong horse and he could smell a genuine character. Jolande would occasionally beg him for a posh one. He would grumble but Jolande would get her way. I enjoyed so much being part of their well-run yard in southern Smithfield, if only for a short while, and seeing their art in passing on a fitting horse, compatible with the capability and personality of their clients.

Gradually, more countries are importing warmbloods and with that the quality of the warmblood horse abroad has vastly improved. The Dutch are now venturing out to countries such as the Emirates, Russia and China. Generally, the people interested are willing to spend good money and make their contacts with top dealers and breeders, whose profit is made for their knowledge and trustworthiness. The horses are admired for their extraordinary quality of movement, their extravagant jumping ability and gradually, as the percentage of thoroughbred in them is soaring higher, also for their boldness going cross-country. In many ways this is a very exciting development, however, I do pray and hope, that these beautiful horses will be loved, admired and cared for the way they deserve and as well as the horses which founded this long success ride to fame.

2

KWPN HISTORY IN A NUTSHELL

Stallion Show in Utrecht in 1961.

In 1887 the first foals were officially registered by regional associations. These associations were financially supported and run, mostly, by farmers, whereas doctors, notaries, vicars and other dignitaries were invited to buy shares in order to subsidize the organized breeding of a more refined horse, a carriage horse capable of swiftly bringing its owner to his destination, a horse that also served a purpose for the artillery. This type of breeding gradually changed around 1920 when another need had to be filled, the breeding of the riding horse. Riding clubs started to spring up in the country; young farmers, soon followed by others, wanted a horse that was more light-footed than its predecessor, still working the land, but gradually replaced by the tractor.

Through the years many associations proceeded to collaborate, which eventually left two studbooks. In 1943 the N.W.P. was formed in the north, with its Groningen horse, whereas earlier, in 1939, the V.L.N. had already established itself involving the rest of the country. Note that this process took place during and despite the Second World War being in full swing, which was extraordinary when you think of it.

The N.W.P. was a closed studbook, only allowing the use of Oldenburg blood based on the rumour that, many years ago, some breeders had left with their Groningen horses for Oldenburg and bred with Oldenburg stock, and therefore, having created a close relationship, some Oldenburg mares were imported in order to be crossed with Groningen stallions.

The V.L.N., which included the Gelderland horse, was an open studbook, allowing other bloodlines, such as Selle-Français and the Anglo-Normand horse.

This was also the time the thoroughbred made its entry. In the past the associations had been hesitant and wanted the process to move more gradually. However, some brave individuals invested privately into the thoroughbred and the results were more than satisfying. After that, the studbooks supported the process and from then on the Dutch Warmblood grew into a different specimen by the year.

As time went on the two types of horses gradually started to look more alike, partly because the V.L.N. still allowed Groningen stallions to be used, and, in 1970, the two studbooks joined forces and the W.P.N. was formed. In 1988, a hundred years after the first foals were registered, the 'K' of 'Koninklijk', meaning 'Royal', was given to the studbook by Queen Beatrix. With that the K.W.P.N., now famous throughout the entire horse world, entered a new era, blossoming as never before.

§

One of the great advantages of the K.W.P.N is that it kept the policy of the old V.L.N. of being an open studbook, unlike for example the Trakehner studbook and also, to some extent, the Selle Français, Hanovarian and Holstein studbooks, which have their restrictions. This allows for all options to be open in order to consistently breed high quality sport horses.

3

STUD, BREEDER AND TRAINER; EACH CAN'T LIVE WITHOUT THE OTHERS

THE FIRST RIDING CLUBS in the Netherlands started to appear just before and during the Second World War. It amazed me time again, when listening to so many different stories, how, despite all the terrible things that happened, the hunger and the fear, people still carried on trying to achieve things and even tried to have some fun.

EARLY DAYS, PROBABLY IN THE FIFTIES, AT
RIDING CLUB 'DE ZEVENSTEEN'.

I guess, from listening to the arguments of my own parents, my mother a little girl in a city, my dad a youngster growing up in the East and more agricultural part of the Netherlands, that life in the country was somewhat less stressful than life in town - but on the other hand, any farmer or person relying on their horse for their livelihood ran the risk for their horse to be taken by the Germans.

After the war, when life gradually took on a more normal pace and with the relief of freedom freshly ingrained into every single person, businesses and agriculture started to grow and with that, for many, wealth grew steadily. The tractor gradually replaced the workhorse and, for many farmers, the opportunity arose to use their mares, now without a job, entirely for breeding riding horses in the hope that this would be profitable.

Oom Hans Vleemingh showing some of his stock.

Initially, most who bred also rode their own horses. More often than not, the breeding started on old-fashioned mixed farms where the main income came from milk and keeping pigs. If the farmers could not ride themselves for whatever reason, there were always sons or daughters who were happy to do so. Also, youngsters from villages and small towns found their way to these farms, begging for a ride. Often those who managed to find their way like that, turned out to be talented and they were certainly driven.

This is exactly how, for example, trainer Roeli Bril found his way into his uncle's coal merchant yard and, using the horses that pulled the coal carts during the week, started his own riding education on a strip of grass in the middle of the small town of Zutphen. When his professional riding career was established, he became crucial to the development of many a great horse and rider, directly and indirectly adding to the success of studs and breeders such as Henk Nijhof and Johan Venderbosch.

Jan Oortveld, son of a baker, was supported by his parents in his desire to become a professional horseman. He had the opportunity to take his formal education at the, then, new and famous equine centre in Deurne in the south of Holland. His youth was very different to most people's because of it and most of his contemporaries would have walked away from such a tough and lonely existence as he lived in his younger years. Jan, as trainer and instructor, has put his stamp on the Dutch horse world with tremendous dedication.

§

This was the beginning of yet another era. Now that many farmers were in the process of fully converting to horse breeding and studs had moved in a similar direction, there was room, no, a great need, for good riders with a decent riding education. The professional rider was now a fact and fully part of the horse breeding and producing business that the Netherlands was creating.

§

The time has come to move on and learn more of the lives and dedication of some of the entrepreneuring horsemen of Gelderland.

4

JOHAN VENDERBOSCH

YOUNG JOHAN WITH HIS PONY LIESJE IN HARNESS
IN FRONT OF THEIR FARMHOUSE

CLOSE TO THE GERMAN BORDER, in 'de Achterhoek', a rural area in Gelderland, farmer Venderbosch was a proud man when he walked around his fields to check the livestock on his fifty-acre farm, 'de Radstake'. The fields were managed well and the stock fencing was in good shape. He liked a tidy yard and so, on Saturday, the broom came out and every corner was swept out meticulously so that everything would look pristine for the Sunday. Sunday was a rest day and family or a friendly neighbour might visit for a cup of coffee, often followed by an *'advocaatje'* for the women and a *'jonkie met suiker'* for the men.

It was a decent-size farm for the area situated on a centuries-old trade route from Germany, hence the fact there was also an ancient tavern on the premises. Although Venderbosch kept some pigs and chickens, the main income came from the tavern and from the milk produced by his thirty-odd dairy cows. There was also a fine team of Groningen work horses and the little pony Liesje, which pulled the cart with the milk churns to the corner of the lane, from where they were collected to go to the milk factory.

Often his young son Johan would play with this pony, teach it tricks, sit on it or tie it to his little sleigh during the winter when the snow had arrived. He was certainly the son of his father and loved the smell of a horse equally, which gave Venderbosch tremendous satisfaction.

§

From early on in his life, from well before the war and before he became a husband and a father, whenever the work was finished for the day farmer Venderbosch would always spend time with the draught horses, even when they'd already been all put away for the night. He would give them an extra brush, talk gently to them or have put their beds to right once more; he would dream of being able to ride properly and he hoped one day to breed a riding horse using his best draught mare.

As soon as there was talk of setting up regional associations in order to organize the breeding of horses in a more professional way, Venderbosch put his name forward so that he could have some input. He had put a lot of thinking time into what he thought was the way forward and wanted his ideas to be used. Like other associations in the country, his association *'De Toekomst'* sold shares to the vicars, doctors and notaries in their area, in the hope that they would grab the opportunity to one day have a smarter and faster horse to pull their carriage because that was their means of transport. It was hoped the more well-off farmers would buy shares as well because the workhorse could also do with some organizing. The studbook VLN was for the Gelderland horse, the finer-framed work horse. The NWP studbook was for the Groningen horse, the stockier of the two, used for the work on the heavy clay ground.

The first stallion to arrive for the association was the Gelderland horse Amburg, an exciting start to a whole new era. From then on, all associations agreed on a universal selection process, with regional grading shows to be held regularly. All information was gathered nationally in order to create much greater control on what farmers were up to with their mares and stallions. Soon, the penny dropped that breeding from a mare without papers had no future and did not make any money, and stallions were cut as soon as their progeny did not perform to the required standards.

§

On Saturdays not just the yard was swept but also all tack got cleaned because often, on Sundays, there would be a carriage-driving show somewhere in the area and Venderbosch would be on his way, often before dawn, with carriage and horse gleaming from tip to toe and Venderbosch in his best suit.

But he still wanted to ride and there were other young farmers with the same aspirations as him; some meetings were organized and soon the riding club 'Varsseveld' was the second official riding club in the country with farmer Venderbosch being one of the founders. All would meet up on their horses for weekly group lessons in a fenced-off piece of land. More riding clubs were formed and soon driving and riding competitions were combined and organized regularly all over the country with a national championship at the end of every year.

§

The war had been over for several years now and young son Johan was growing up fast, helping his dad on the farm after school. The little old pony was retired out in the field with the calves because it wasn't needed any more for shifting the milk churns. The tractor, by now a common sight in the fields, did all of that rather than the loyal workhorse.

Just after he passed his exams, when he was fifteen years old, his father sent Johan to international show-jump rider, Troop Captain Gruppelaar for several months. Venderbosch was extremely keen for Johan to have every possible chance to develop his horse skills and Gruppelaar had a name for being an excellent teacher. This was an exciting time for Johan because he was allowed to travel with the horses on the train to many different international shows all over Europe and the train journeys were nearly as exciting as the shows themselves. When going to Paris or to Marseille their coach had to be reconnected to another train. Normally this would happen with a big bang, enough to throw the horses over. Hence why a specially assigned young lad was instructed to stick his head out of the carriage and call out, 'Attention! cheveaux!.' This was to ensure that the person in charge of the change-over of the carriages would take care and slow the procedure down as much as possible.

Johan had to work hard because 'the old Grup', as the lads used to call him when he was out of earshot, liked things perfect. He was a typical cavalryman, extremely punctual, well-organized and liked things spotless, with his white glove often sending the lads back to the brush. Still, young Johan had a wonderful time and came home full of stories that his father loved listening to.

§

Johan was eighteen years old when he lost his dad but there wasn't much time to dwell on this sudden tragedy because from that very day he had to run the entire business by himself. His responsibilities were huge: there was not only the dairy herd and the tavern, but there were also the broodmares and their offspring, which had become a significant part of the farm, and, on top of all that, Johan took on the position of his dad within association *'De Toekomst'*, which was heading for turbulent times.

For a while voices had been going up within the organisation about the need for them to make big decisions in order to try and add yet more quality to the Dutch horse, since it was a fact that the draught horse was not needed on the land anymore and the sport of dressage and show-jumping was becoming not only more popular but also more demanding. Meetings were filled with hot discussions between members who wanted to take it slowly by carefully adding Normandy blood, and the group for whom Johan was the spokesman, who wanted to leap into the unknown and introduce the thoroughbred. Johan had done his homework and saw that specially in Germany many different breeds had already done so. As a matter of fact, well before the Trakehner studbook closed its doors to other bloodlines, King Wilhelm von Preussen had demanded that the Trakehner horse be crossed with thoroughbreds from as early as the eighteenth century, in order to produce a spirited and powerful cavalry horse - and very successfully too.

Johan was particularly interested in the French thoroughbred. Like Germany, France had studs owned and run by the state for its cavalry. Show-jumping had been a popular sport in France for quite a while and the *Cadre Noir* was a very fine example, not only of excellent horsemanship but also of the extremely high standard of the breeding of a more modern and quality horse.

At one such meeting the general consent was that if Johan wanted to breed with a thoroughbred stallion, he was on his own. The association was not willing to take the financial risk. If this worried Johan, his actions didn't show it. First he tried to get the stallion Lucky Boy. There were a few other breeders with similar ideas and all who were interested had to make a silent bid after the stallion was shown in hand. Johan's bid turned out to be the second highest and so he missed out.

His search went on and during this time he found something else. He was in his early twenties by now and he knew that he wanted for Gerrie, the lovely girl he had been dating for a while, to be his wife. They settled into their life together on the farm and Gerrie became his loyal supporter, part of all major decisions and, in due course, their three children, Henriette, Robert and André, arrived. Together they also dared to invest into the somewhat outdated tavern and turned it into an extremely successful restaurant and catering business.

GERRIE IN FOLK COSTUME TOGETHER WITH JOHAN AT THE OPENING OF A NEW PART OF THEIR RESTAURANT AND CATERING BUSINESS.

JOHAN WITH HIS SMALL CHILDREN WITH THE DAIRY COWS AT AN AGRICULTURAL SHOW AT 'DE RADSTAKE'.

§

When Johan got word of a thoroughbred stallion in the northeast of the country with a decent race record, he decided to drive up and take a look. The dark bay stallion was owned by a private yard that was willing to sell. He liked the stallion but requested to see some of his offspring if possible. He was told to wait in the foyer and, rather to his astonishment, after a little wait the door opened and up the small staircase came three youngsters, happily nosing around and after some minutes they were guided out again. Venderbosch could not believe what he had just seen and also sadly had not been able to see much of their movement, but this was all he had to make his decision on. He told the owner he wanted to go home to think things over; at the end of the day it was a big investment.

He couldn't wait to get back to tell Gerrie about it. They talked things over and because it just so happened to be his birthday that week, somehow it seemed appropriate to make the phone call there and then. On that very evening, after another talk with Gerrie, he called, failed to convince the owner to take a bit off the price and bit the bullet. He walked back into the living room in a haze and nodded. All the waiting birthday guests gave a big cheer and it turned into a very jolly evening.

Pericles arrived and that was the beginning of a wonderful time. He turned out to be the kindest possible horse. As soon as Johan started riding him he realized he had something very special. With his previous owners Pericles had found switching from the racetrack to the show-jump ring easy and Johan soon realized how extremely talented this horse was. Johan loved competing Pericles and Pericles had no problem combining a competition career with his job as a sire, covering up to six mares a day. He loved going for a hack and, when out on the lanes, was such a gentleman that he never made life awkward for his rider. He soon became a hugely influential sire and his fame spread far and wide.

§

By now Johan had lured an interesting man to come and work for him. It took some doing; Johan Freriks, with the bristly long sideburns and old-fashioned to the bone, was a man of few words and was not so fond of all this new, sleek, horse stuff. But still, Freriks's reputation as a true horseman had travelled all over the region and Johan really liked him. Above all, Johan needed someone on the lorry whom he could fully trust with his stallions and he knew Freriks fitted the bill. In those days it was common practice for the stallions to be on the lorry for most of the day during the breeding season, visiting the farmers who had called to say their mare was in season.

In order to keep Freriks happy Johan eventually bought a young driving stallion that this quite stubborn man would like. Vizier did not stay long but served his purpose and Freriks became crucial to Johan's success. He had such a knack with horses. The stallions respected him because he respected them in return and they sensed they were safe with him. Freriks never moaned about the long hours on the road because they gave him a sense of freedom which he rather liked.

§

In the year of 1970, by which time all the associations had gradually ceased to exist, the VLN and NWP fused into the WPN studbook. All investors in the two associations were given their money back and Johan was now completely independent. The breeding had always been a venture based on the desire to improve the breeding standard and not for increasing one's wealth. As a sign of appreciation the associations would probably give an investor a present for when there was a celebration to be had, a silver wedding anniversary for instance, but now the books were closed for a new era to begin.

THE WHOLE FAMILY WITH ROSETTES AND A VERY PROUD AND HAPPY MOTHER GERRIE.

§

The horse breeding business had now fully established itself and the horse itself became more precious and valuable, which caused for a change to take place in the veterinary world. In the east of Holland veterinarian Mulder may have been the first to set up a specialized equine clinic. Johan knew him quite well and one day had a phone call with Mulder who sounded quite excited about a stallion in France he thought Johan should go and see. He was standing at a beautiful stud in Normandy owned by Lefevre, renowned for his good taste in a horse. Mulder and Johan were joined for the trip by a young lady who was an acquaintance of Troop Captain Gruppelaar. She was an important asset because she spoke French and they did not.

Every year Lefevre bought a huge number of foals, which were kept in groups in huge fields for the year. During the following autumn the youngsters likely to stand a chance would be produced for the stallion show. The best Lefevre would generally keep for his own stud, but he was always willing to sell if the money was right.

It was the stallion Le Mexico whom Johan fell for. After the viewing Lefevre was in the habit of offering his prospective buyers a small and quite strong drink, but this was not for Johan because he wasn't much of a boozer. And he did not need a drink in order to know that this extremely good-moving stallion was for him. The deal was made and off they went back to the hotel. While Johan was making his way to his room, the owner of the hotel hurried after him and told him he was to move into a different room. Instructions from Lefevre: Johan collected his travel bag and walked into his new room, the bridal suite!

That same year the stallions Liguster and L'Espoir were bought by breeders from Holland and all appeared together at the stallion grading show. Liguster won the championship, L'Espoir was third but Le Mexico had a disappointing second premium. Johan felt disgusted and hurt, however, after the performance test, things looked up because Le Mexico won the championship and the other two, although still successful, in the long run made far less of an impact on the breeding scene than Le Mexico. Johan could not believe his luck and life was good.

§

Baker Bleekman from nearby had been visiting occasionally for a while because he was a fervent breeder and liked Johan's stallions. On Sundays Bleekman would pick up his young nephew Edward in his car and they would do a 'little round' as the baker would call it. They would visit all the different studs in the area: Te Luggenhorst, Borghuis, Kelholt-Weerink, to name but a few. Occasionally they would go further afield because Bleekman wasn't shy of travelling his broodmares to the west or the north of the country if a certain stallion took his fancy. He really liked the stallions belonging to Tonny van de Koppel in the Betuwe, and Wiepke van de Lageweg in Friesland was paid the odd visit as well. It went both ways because Wiepke also liked some of the baker's mares.

Venderbosch was the yard they would end up at most regularly however. Young Edward soon managed to find his way onto the lorry with the stallions. Freriks quite liked the lad so off they went together visiting the farms. Initially Edward was just a passenger, watching eagerly how Freriks went to work. On arrival in a yard, Freriks would double-check with the farmer which stallion should be taken off the lorry and the mare was then led to a little hatch on the side of the lorry. With the stallions getting excited, the mare would show by 'blinking', as was the expression, whether she was ready. Still, this could be false alarm and therefore, to be on the safe side, any tricky mare would be hobbled. A rope tied around one of her fetlocks on the hind leg would be attached to a rope around her neck which made it virtually impossible for her to kick out and injure the stallion. The desired stallion was unloaded from the side ramp and the dance would begin. Edward was full of respect at how

Freriks played this game. It was potentially an extremely dangerous job, but Freriks kept a cool head at all times, seemingly unfazed by the whole exercise. If unsuccessful they would have to come back either the next day or when the mare was having her next season. They were long days, leaving early in the morning and in the midst of a season not back before ten or eleven o'clock at night.

It would happen occasionally that they turned up and the farmer was nowhere to be found. If they knew their way around they helped themselves. The older mares were especially easy because they knew the game. Freriks would tie the mare to a fence and she would patiently stand there for the stallion to do his job.

The stallion Profeet, a son of Liberto, was often on the lorry as the teaser because he was not wanted that often. If he did have a job, it was lethal both for the person leading the stallion and the handler of the mare because Profeet would barely know which end of the mare to jump on. The legs of the madly screaming stallion would be flying and both men would be relieved when he was safely back on the lorry again.

Freriks liked passing on his skills to his eager young friend. As a matter of fact, he would never let on but it made him a little bit proud and happy, in a strange sort of way.

§

Baker Bleekman had a good eye and loved the modern horse. For a while now, every time he visited, he could not stop bugging Johan to buy a stallion, which, according to him, would come for sale as the risk of inbreeding in the area increased by the year. The Holstein x Trakehner stallion, Amor, had been with the oldest association of all, the 'Schagen', in the north west of the country for some seven years. At the stallion show the stunning bay had conquered the hearts of all present. Baker Bleekman had some contacts because he had regularly gone there with some of his mares. Johan knew he would have to spend a lot of money but in the end baker Bleekman won. His fever rubbed off on Johan, the contact was made and Amor became part of 'De Radstake' stud where he would stay until the very end of his life.

But the state he was in when he arrived! Whereas stallions were always and at all times presented fully groomed and shining from top to bottom, Amor seemed untouched for quite a while; his mane were in a sorry state as if not pulled in a long while. They found out soon enough: Amor did not at all want to be touched around his head. Was he head shy? Freriks was left to find out. It took one short but strict telling-off and Freriks was able to do the job. It did take a man like Freriks, though, to understand that if you start near the shoulder and work towards the head, rather than the usual way where one starts near the head, Amor was just about able to come up with the patience to stick it. It was clear from the beginning: Amor would take you on and battle any confrontation, but was always ready to reach a compromise.

He loved grey mares or mares with a foal at foot; he'd be done in no time. But black mares or mares smelling like pigs he would not go near… unless… often there was the small grey pony on the lorry and when Amor had dug his heels in, this little thing only had to be walked of the ramp and the stallion would quickly change his mind.

Johan realized that this character trait definitely showed in the offspring and would put a halter on Amor's youngsters sooner than he normally did. They were certainly feisty, but they did show that same grit in their work, especially in the show-jump ring.

One day, when they turned up at a farm and the farmer went to get the mare from her stable, Freriks told fifteen-year-old Edward to get Amor of the lorry. Edward couldn't believe his ears; had he heard this right? Nervous, but keeping a cool head, he did as he was told and served his teacher proud. Little did he know that one day he would be doing this job all by himself…

§

Once again, Doctor Mulder, by now retired as WPN veterinarian, turned up in Johan's yard highly excited. He vowed that he had seen the very stallion Johan had been looking for quite a while. Cadmus had not only run successfully on the flat, but also over hurdles. Johan could not resist Mulder's excitement because, for a long time, he had badly wanted a thoroughbred that had raced over hurdles. He was of the strong opinion that this would be a perfect combination with the type of mares he was dealing with.

Johan went to see Cadmus and when Mr. Nuy from Castle 'Boxbergen' showed the stallion proudly in hand, he fell in love with this stunningly moving and spirited stallion. The strong shoulder with that unusually expressive movement in front! A little long in the hind leg, but the power it created was extraordinary. Johan was very excited to make a lease arrangement with Mr. Nuy for Cadmus.

§

It was Edward's birthday and his friends had arrived; Edward was missing however. Cadmus was going to arrive at 'De Radstake' and baker Bleekman and other friends, who were always expected to be present when a new important arrival was due, were waiting for Freriks to turn up with the new asset but by the time they were led to the stable to see Cadmus, they couldn't see anything. A mist had formed. They could barely see each other because a fog was swirling around the stable light. Cadmus had obviously not quite taken to his new environment and needed some more time to settle in.

Edward arrived rather late for his own birthday party finding a happy gang of friends having a very good time.

Freriks in his favourite outfit trying his very best to present the stallion Cadmus, who hated standing still.

Despite his hot disposition Cadmus was liked by many and popular as a sire. He had his own little lorry because he was extremely dominant and did not like sharing with the other stallions. Nephew Edward, now in his late teens and well-trained by Freriks, drove the stallions regularly to the mares by himself. One day, at one of the stallion shows, Edward was made to stay in the little lorry with Cadmus to keep the impatient stallion settled and, unfortunately, Johan had accidentally locked the jockey door. As the horse traffic increased Cadmus became more and more unruly. Edward, not easily scared, decided he needed to get out as too many legs were flying in all directions but found himself locked in. By the time Johan came to check on them Edward was very white around the nose and made sure this never happened to him again.

Cadmus had such a great racing record that he had been accepted by the WPN without having to do the performance test.

He did have to show his offspring, though and because they were unanimously magnificent movers that did not worry Johan. The first two lots had been greatly appreciated by the judges. The third year the ground was very wet because there had been torrential rain for weeks and Johan didn't see it coming. He understood the thoroughbred better than most and he could see and understood why the youngsters were holding back a bit, because this is what a racehorse does in order not to hurt itself. The jury could not accept this and Cadmus was thrown out as a sire, leaving Johan devastated and furious. As a matter of fact, he waited several months to cool down before he took pen and paper to write to the WPN with his point of view - because how did the previous two reports square with the one he just received? It did not make any sense! The leading judge, Mr. Binsbergen, was a competent and honest man. In his responding letter he was able to admit that this could possibly have been a mistake but there was no turning things around, the truth was in the future; that was how Mr. Binsbergen finished his written apology.

Johan was touched by the fact that the judge had made the effort, though this was a meagre comfort to Johan. He paid off what he owed Mr. Nuy and soon Cadmus went back to France. Only a few years after his departure Cadmus died in the harness when covering a mare.

Several years later at the WPN stallion show at Utrecht, judge Binsbergen tapped Johan on the shoulder. 'You were right, we made a mistake,' he said.

§

It is 2015 and 'De Radstake' has grown from a fifty-acre dairy farm into a 140-acre stud. If the old farmer Venderbosch was able to see this achievement he would be so very proud of his son Johan because these were his dreams and his aspirations.

EARLY DAYS: THE DAIRY HERD IN THEIR BARN.

Looking back, Johan feels strongly that he had the tide with him: he knew what he wanted. It all began with a sound and uncomplicated horse for the general hobby rider. With the thoroughbred the Dutch horse gradually became the top sport horse admired for its capabilities the world all over. Johan describes the conversion of the Dutch workhorse with the use of the thoroughbred as: 'a little bit of liquor tastes good and is nice as a mixed drink, but too much will kill you'.

He wishes that the trend to want too much too soon could be brought to a grinding halt. The demands of the KWPN performance tests need to be in context with the strength of the horse at that very young age. To his mind it can ruin a horse's prospects, causes unnecessary lameness bordering on being not animal-friendly. The fact that these days a stallion can be recognized later in life because of his competition record is a huge improvement.

His great love and respect for the horse will always be his motivator and, at the time of writing, together with his wife Gerrie, Johan is happy to advise and oversee how his daughter

Henriette and son André are carrying on - and 'De Radstake' is as successful as ever.

§

Baker Bleekman was the driving force behind the life-size beautiful bronze statue of Amor, the stallion who changed the Dutch breeding world, which stands proudly at the entrance to stud 'De Radstake'. Three miniatures were made of this statue, of which one is now in the home of Edward Bleekman, left to him by his uncle.

THE STATUE OF AMOR IN FRONT OF STUD 'DE RADSTAKE'.

§

Edward has his own successful stud in Cullompton, in the county of Devon in England, together with his wife Clarissa, to whom he was introduced by Roeli Bril some twenty-odd years ago at the international three-day event at Boekelo in Twente, in the north east of Holland. Clissy, as most know her, was an extremely competent event rider and competed for England and Holland. At the time of writing, two of their three daughters, all great riders and having dual nationality, compete for the Netherlands. Several of the horses the Bleekman daughters compete are by the famous event rider Mark Todd's stallion May Hill, who, during his working life, stood at Whorridge Stud.

EDWARD AND CLISSY BLEEKMAN IN FRONT
OF THEIR FARMHOUSE IN DEVON.

During the years several stallions traveled from stud 'De Radstake' to Whorridge Stud, Karandasj, the black show-jump stallion being one of them. That just shows how strong the bond is between both studs and, what's more, an enduring friendship.

5

HENK NIJHOF

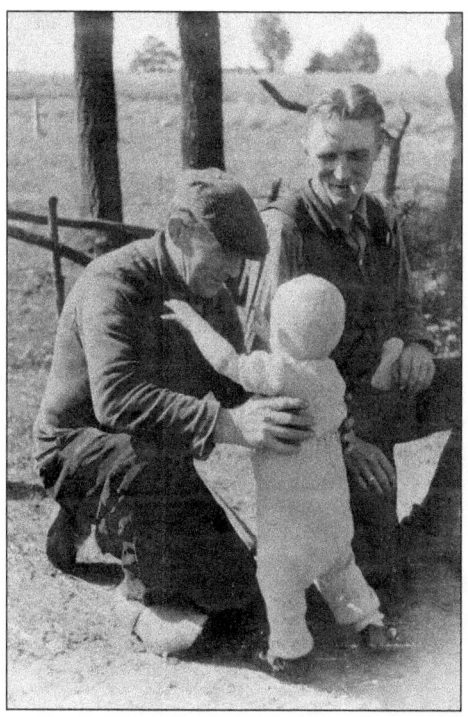

THREE GENERATIONS NIJHOF.

GRANDFATHER HENDRIK-JAN NIJHOF farmed eight acres. By the time Henk was born at the end of the Second World War, his father had managed to buy another sixteen acres and they were milking twelve cows by hand, morning and evening. They had some pigs that were fed barley and the scraps from the kitchen; chickens and a rooster ran free in the barnyard and, of course, there was also the vegetable garden. It was a small farm but it supplied them with everything they needed as long as all pitched in and worked hard. Grandfather Nijhof had a keen interest in his work horses because he did not just breed in order to replace the older ones but wanted to improve them, and he shared the general desire to organize the breeding in his area more effectively. It was a great day for all on the farm when, in 1946, their stallion Heraut was approved by the studbook and this was the beginning of the Nijhof success. When Heraut was eventually sold to one of the regional associations for the vast amount of 45,000 guilders, that was a huge breakthrough, to say the least.

The stallion Heraut, who was approved in 1946.

Still, money had to be made in every possible way because the outgoings were high and, for a time, when poultry sold well in the Far East, a little extra cash was made through increasing that side of things, always maintaining the family policy that money never went to luxury but was always ploughed back into the farm.

Henk was an only child and doted on by his parents. The fact that he loved horses was a bonus because his parents were keen horse lovers themselves. As a matter of fact, long after the neighbours had tractors, Henk's dad stubbornly walked behind the plough with his horses. Henk was only ten when he joined his dad working the fields, watching the hamstrings of the two hardworking horses tighten and stretch in a steady rhythm as they worked the field back and forth. Soon Henk was able to go by himself and loved walking next to the newly turned furrow with its fresh soily smell and a colour so very alive.

FATHER JAN NIJHOF WITH A HEAVILY LADEN CART.

Despite occasionally being a bit put off when the next door farmer turned his tractor up the farm drive, having finished his field whereas they were only halfway, they delayed the decision to change things as long as possible. There was something so very wholesome about being together with those trustworthy and loyal horses, their big, solid bodies all steamed up from their hard labour, about bringing them home and, instead of turning the key for the engine to shut down, having to spend a long time washing them or rubbing them down with straw in order to clean and cool their hot skin. No matter how tired, it felt good to feed and drench them before the men allowed themselves to have their own tea, going back before bedtime to see that they were all right for the night with the tiny stable light throwing its shadows from the thick oak beams and some of the horses lying down, others still finishing up their last bits of hay or chewing lazily on some bedding. After a hard day's work this was Henk's most contented moment and he longed for it always.

The tractor only arrived when their interest in horses began to shift towards the riding horse. When Henk was thirteen his dad bought him an experienced competition horse and Henk joined the local riding club where, several years later, he shone at show-jumping with Brammetje. He was now competing regularly with success and his devotion and riding skills brought him to national competition level. His dad not only loved watching his son but saw another opportunity. He started buying young horses for Henk because, by the time Henk got them to jump well, they sold well. This gave a bit of spare cash which more than supported a sport which otherwise would have been difficult to afford. They were farmers and therefore were used to turn their animals or whatever else they produced into a profit and, although they loved them, it was no different for their horses and it was accepted and understood that when money could be made, the horse would move to its next home.

§

Life became hectic with the farm work and competition riding not always running kindly next to one another. There were many more horses in the yard, which needed a very different care from the work horses. Henk was in the last few years of agricultural college which took up a fair bit of time as well. Harvest time was particularly tough. Ready hay on a beautiful dry day wouldn't wait for college or a competition. Bales had first to be pitched on the flatbed trailer, with the stack growing higher and higher, and then unloaded into the barn attic, back-breaking work. If the next day was a competition day, Henk's sore muscles had a hard time being as supple as they should have been in order to twist and turn from one fence to another.

At only twenty-one years old Henk experienced a severe back injury and his riding career was over. Not only was it a tough setback for their growing business of buying and selling horses but from now on Henk was also consistently in pain and had to make some major decisions. There was no time to dwell on things and he threw himself into all kinds of courses. He became a judge, a show-jump course builder and an instructor and soon began giving courses for judges and training on-coming instructors himself. He brought the local riding club a national victory with their squadron team.

But foremost he decided to share his dad's interest in breeding. More broodmares were bought. At one point he had his eye on a dark bay mare in foal by the stallion Talisman, a stallion he very much liked. He bought the mare and when her colt foal grew up to be a good-looking stallion, the whole family was so very proud. Unfortunately, this turned out to be a mistake; when Henk spotted a good horse he saw no colour, but the breeders wanted only chestnuts and the bay stallion was completely ignored by them. It was a tough lesson but also one of the very few mistakes Henk made because his gut feeling proved him right most times - and the business kept growing.

Henk wanted more. He saw stallions he liked and, although irritated that he did not have a suitable yard to keep them properly, this did not stop him from buying the first one. After failing to outbid farmer Borghuis in silent auction on the thoroughbred stallion Lucky Boy, Henk managed to lay his hands on Lucky Boy's first son, Naturel. In 1979 a delighted young Henk won the championship at the national stallion show with Naturel.

This was the beginning of what eventually would become the philosophy of the Dutch Warmblood studbook but at that time was a personal and extremely enterprising experiment. Henk and a few others wanted the thoroughbred to enter the world of the Dutch breeding fraternity. Their Dutch horses had the power and the willingness to work hard and Henk strongly believed that the thoroughbred would add the brains and the agility needed in order to become a better, if not the best, sports horse. Henk dared to stick his neck out and look across the border. He started to visit stallion shows in Germany and not only made connections with studs there but also managed to make himself welcome in several yards in England. When he went on his travels, his parents, although getting older, held the fort and made sure all ran smoothly.

A PROUD HENK NIJHOF WITH THE STALLION NATUREL,
CHAMPION AT THE STALLION SHOW IN 1979.

§

Henk had another conviction. He believed that, just as in school, you had to make a choice at some point what to study in order to specialize and, like with cows of which some are bred to produce milk and others to become meat, also horses have to be bred to specialize into either dressage or show-jumping rather than be a little bit good at everything. This was how he and his father laid the base for their stud.

The smouldering problem was that they were still not set up as a proper stud as yet. Although gradually having grown smaller in number, the cows were still there and, amongst them, mares and foals were all over the place. A lot needed to change and it would mean a huge investment.

So, although Henk had bought Naturel he was not able to keep him. A buyer was found in Van Tuyl who liked what Henk was doing and decided to invest in him. By now Henk was regularly buying promising young colts in order to produce them for the stallion show in 's-Hertogenbosch, which took place in February. It was organized just before the stallions would turn three. They had to pass the in hand phase in order to be qualified for the hundred day test, during which time they were backed and tested on their jumping and dressage ability. It was not an easy time of the year to prepare the young horses. The ground was either sodden or frozen rock-hard as it so often was in the midst of winter. The preparation all had to be done in the fields and even the best-behaved two year-old stallion could be a handful. Henk ignored all that and kept on doing what he had to do in order to make it work; one year, winter was so unforgiving they had to abandon the fields and his parents happily allowed him to move the training to their very tidy garden. His mother never flinched as the grass got gradually churned into mud and plants and bushes were demolished. As a matter of fact, both she and her husband loved watching the spectacle from her living-room window. In spring the grass was reseeded and everything was put back as it was before and, with several stallions having passed the test, it had all been worth it.

It was a little later that year that Henk saw Roemer and fell for this powerful stallion in a big way. Herman Hahnen, who was his contact, said it was not possible to sell him because he was already accepted by the Oldenburg studbook and they wouldn't let him go, but Henk persevered and persevered. The stallion kept him awake! In the end Hahnen told him he could have two-year-old Roemer for 40.000 deutsche marks if he bought another one as well. When Henk broke this news to his father it went very quiet. The look on his father's face told him everything: if this was a mistake they would lose all they possessed, the farm, their livestock, the lot. After another week of sleepless nights Henk pushed on. It would turn out to be their big break.

§

Henk had just finished building an engine-driven horse walker, a very novel way to give horses exercise without having to be personally involved. He did it all by himself and he was very proud of it. He watched with satisfaction as Roemer and Rinaldo, the first ones in, took to it well and seemed to be happy and safe walking in circles, each in their own separate area, gently being pushed along. This would save an enormous amount of work in order to produce the young stallions and add terrifically to their fitness level.

Roemer, being a foreign horse, was not allowed to win the Graaf van Lindenburg trophy and Henk was disappointed he wasn't placed higher at the stallion show but his other stallion Rinaldo won. Even so, Roemer won the hearts of many and especially the heart of Henk van Tuyl who not only bought him for 200.000 guilders, but also invested in Rinaldo.

§

The business took up a lot of his time but Henk did manage to find time to meet Aleid, a stalwart farmer's daughter who worked as a nurse. She was not at all interested in horses but, despite that, they made a good pair and got married. During the next few years they had their two children, a son called Henk, named after his father, and their daughter Jeanette. Like many other children, neither one of them took much notice of their father's business. Henk Junior was more interested in the few cows that were left and as time went on Aleid recognized the farmer in her son and often sent him to her brother who had a farm nearby and who was not married with no children of his own.

§

With mixed feelings the whole of the family saw their last cows walk onto the lorry. The herd had gradually diminished over the years and as the ramp of the cattle lorry closed for the last time, they were now formally a stud. It was the end of an era but also very exciting and, although father Nijhof worried about the financial side with all its unknown factors, for Henk things felt less complicated. He was young and ready to take a risk or two, trusting his choices and gut feeling. The fact that by now he was buying and selling horses to people who always came back for more and were always willing to pay what it took to use his good eye for a horse, gave him the freedom to be a bit more adventurous. He knew that his parents loved what he did and were very proud of him. He realized also that being an only child had put him in a privileged position.

§

In the early eighties veterinarian Jan Greve had settled nearby with his veterinary practice and Henk and he got on well. They had a similar interest and started to make trips together. Normandy was visited - where they found the stallion Versailles. The Dutch breeders did not take to him but the Swiss did, so a deal was made and off Versailles went to yet another part of Europe.

One day the phone rang and Henk was told that there was a suitable young stallion in Oldenburg that he should come and see. He quickly called his friend Jan and a few days later they were on their way. It was at stud Hahnenmoor in Fürstenau, belonging to Professor Kuwert. Professor Kuwert was well known for having discovered the vaccine for rabies, a big problem on the continent; he also had a passion for horses and his estate near Essen was famous for the quality of the many mares, foals, youngsters and stallions he possessed.

Having driven a long way, the two friends were disappointed at being shown a stallion neither of them fancied. When the man who had shown them the stallion led him back to his stable, they asked him whether there was anything else worth seeing and the man said there was a small, two-year-old stallion who hadn't passed the inspection of the studbook. Henk and Jan decided that they would like to see him.

'Jan, we've got to have that little pipsqueak.' Henk was completely smitten from the moment the wee stallion soared over the first fence in a way Henk had never seen done before. Ears pricked at all times, jumping with a style and vigour without ever getting flustered, it was something else! Henk knew his breeding lines and these were very good. There was just no way back. With hearts beating faster and even when the asking price turned out to be the rather large sum of 15.000 guilders, they could not drive home without having bought him.

So the deal was done and they returned excited about their joint ownership of this young and promising stallion. A week later, Henk went with his young neighbour Wim to collect him. The loading went fine and off they drove but they had not got very far on the motorway when the car became near uncontrollable from the shaking of the trailer. Henk tried frantically to stay steady. He steered to the side and as soon as they got out they saw the head of the young horse coming through the roof of the trailer and, when they opened the jockey door, the situation turned out to be even worse because the young stallion's front legs were over the chest bar and the poor stallion was turning himself inside out. Being beside the motorway with the traffic roaring by, this was potentially a very dangerous situation. Somehow, after several failed attempts, they managed to get the chest bar undone and the young horse came crashing down scrambling frantically to stay on his legs. They managed to calm him down and checked him over as well as they possibly could in the cramped space. He tore some skin near his eye but otherwise they couldn't see anything major. For the rest of the journey young Wim was made to stay with the young horse in the trailer to keep him quiet. If there was a problem, he would put a stick through the little window on the side of the trailer so Henk would stop and hopefully settle things down again.

Henk drove off very carefully and they embarked on a very tedious and slow trip home. As things stayed quiet, he started to worry whether the stallion would come of the trailer safe and sound. He started to think about the vast amount of money he and his friend, Jan Greve, had spent. They might have already lost it. Nearing the farm, Henk felt dead tired but relieved to have at least got that far and, eventually, the young stallion came off the trailer reasonably quiet - together with young Wim who was very relieved to be out of his temporary imprisonment.

And the beautiful little 'Voltaire' turned out to be sound and settled in well.

The preparations for the stallion show with Voltaire went smoothly, however the judges' panel was not so impressed. It did not amuse Henk when Voltaire only just made it through the inspection as the fifteenth stallion from the fifteen that were accepted for the next phase. Judge Van Veen called it 'a present' which upset

Henk even more. He knew he had a good stallion and wanted for everybody to see that. And he was right; Voltaire kept on growing and never disappointed in any way. He soon became famous. Henk van Tuyl desperately wanted him, France offered 1,000,000. But Henk wouldn't budge; Voltaire was not for sale. There was one small problem, though: Voltaire had super-quality sperm, but there wasn't enough of it to meet the demand. Fortunately, artificial insemination was on its way and was soon to be accepted as the way to go.

§

Artificial insemination had already been used for quite a few years for cattle. Soon after, experiments with AI for horses followed. There were some wild stories. For example, one about a veterinarian with a friend, who wanted to try to get his mare in foal without the hassle of driving her to the stud. Together they drove to the other side of Belgium, a trip of well over three hours, in order to collect some sperm from a stallion. The veterinarian sped back whereas the friend in the passenger's seat had the tedious job of twisting and turning the test tube for the entire three-hour return drive in order to keep it alive. In hindsight they wondered if it would have been easier to have loaded the mare and driven her up there after all. But it did produce a foal and by the time this foal was born, techniques had advanced at such speed that AI was in common use in the professional breeding world. It solved many problems. Most of all, the life of the stallions improved no end; they did not have to travel anymore and the risk of being kicked during the act was a thing of the past, both for the stallion and the handler.

Later, when France had perfected the method of frozen sperm, it got even better. Frozen sperm was an advantage in every way and particularly for the thoroughbred sire used for the warmblood studbooks. It had gradually become obvious that not all thoroughbred stallions were consistent as far as their fertility was concerned - the explanation being that a thoroughbred was bred for speed and not for sperm.

Also, now the stallions were able to have a competition season without interruption. This meant business!

§

Henk was in his mid-forties by now and, after many doctor's visits for his continuing back problem, one day he saw an unusual sight when visiting Jan Greve at his veterinary centre. A chap he'd met before at Jan's was carrying a large white rabbit into Jan's operating theatre. The man had hands as big as coal shovels. Henk asked Jan what was going on, knowing full and well Jan only dealt with horses, and Jan told him with a grin that the man with the huge hands was a neurologist who wanted to find out more about hernias in backs. He would create a hernia in the poor rabbit's back and then proceed to try to fix it. Back home, Henk could not let go of the image of the man and the big white rabbit. A few days later he called him for an appointment and soon after he was operated on.

Twenty years after he injured himself, he was without pain.

§

Henk Jr. had been to Wales for a practical farming experience and, once back home, hoped to settle down at his single uncle's farm where he had already spent so much time. This was not to be. His uncle was not quite as single as he used to be; he had started to date a 'strange lady from the west of the country' and she was not at all interested in having Henk about. Henk came back home and although it always seemed that his one and only interest had been agriculture, he developed a gradual but keen interest in his dad's passion for horses. Henk Sr. was pleasantly surprised and loved passing his knowledge on to his son. It didn't take long before Henk Jr. started to develop his own ideas and opinions were passed back and forth between the two of them, propelling the business into another gear yet again.

In the meantime, daughter Jeanette had become a private secretary and worked for several ministers, even spending some time in 'het torentje', the unusual prime minister's office in a little tower in The Hague and part of the oldest House of Parliament in the world still in use. She had thrived learning her languages and felt an urge to spread her wings by taking on a job in another country. Henk Sr. was not excited about this. His business could do with her knowledge of languages because they had started to sell horses and sperm all over the world. Ever since the French had developed the method for freezing sperm successfully, other countries including Holland had cottoned on. With all these new developments many more regulations were imposed and the administrational burden had increased beyond belief.

Father and daughter made a deal: Henk Sr. paid Jeanette for a year travelling around the world and after that she would become part of the business.

§

Every time the stud made some money it went into a new shed or to replenish the young stock. Occasionally a bigger investment would be made in a new stallion. One day, a last-minute tip when he was already on his way to Stanstead airport to return to Holland, made Henk turn around to see a young stallion. When he arrived there was nobody in the yard and time was ticking but over one of the top doors Henk saw this horse with the most beautiful head and neck. He knew that if the rest of his body was just as good looking, he had to have him. He finally found somebody who told him he had to wait until after the inspection. Henk only just made his plane, frustrated not to have made a deal, but his patience paid off. Some months later he bought the stallion and sold him on for a vast profit to Oldenburg.

Sometimes he did not get his way. Only some years ago, at the Fontainebleau show, Henk saw a stallion which he liked very much. It wasn't the most beautiful animal to look at, but what a jump and such a fantastic attitude! He knew the lady who owned him and approached her in order to find out whether she would sell. The lady wanted 600,000 euros for her share, whereas the other share would still have to be paid to her Italian partner. This kept him awake for nights on end. The spark had leaped and Henk was not a happy man. He could not easily accept that this horse wasn't for him. Soon after, the nephew of the King of Morocco entered the show-jump arena on this very animal, much to Henk's dismay.

§

HENK SR., HIS DAD AND A YOUNG HELPER IN THE
FIELD WITH THEIR MARES AND FOALS.

When land came up for sale in his area, Henk would jump at it; one could never own enough land. The small eight-acre farm 'Zandman' of Henk Sr.'s grandfather, has grown into an internationally renowned stud with two hundred acres of land. The names of the stallions Roemer, Voltaire and later Heartbreaker and Clinton, just to name a few, are known all over the world.

Henk is gradually sitting back a bit more and allows his son and daughter the space his parents, just as proud and supportive of him as he is now of his children, gave him when he wanted and needed it. He still makes a yearly trip to France in order to see how the breeding industry is developing in the country where he found so many good stallions, and he loves going out and visiting his clients on their studs and farms, taking the scanner, together with his good friend veterinarian Jan Breukink, who has helped him set up their own veterinary unit. Advice was, and is, his strong point and he always enjoys helping clients to make good decisions.

Later in the day, the two friends might just share a glass of wine together, remembering the old days but not yet ready to stop dreaming of the future and, of course, always with reality clearly in mind. Henk, who was one of the first to mix the thoroughbred with the Dutch horse, wants to keep adding some of this blood to the modern Dutch Warmblood.

His philosophy remains that a little bit of poison can be turned into medicine providing it's not too much.

6

JAN OORTVELD

Jan Oortveld with his beloved show-jumper El Capone.

Baker Oortveld and his wife were a hard-working couple running their business in the village of Aerdt in the 'Achterhoek' in Gelderland. While their children were growing up during the fifties and sixties of the previous century, they became part of the work force as soon as they came home from school each day; it was the only way to make ends meet. There were five of them: two boys and three girls. Whenever baker Oortveld somehow managed to get some spare time, he spent it with his Shetland ponies, which he kept in a nearby field. He owned nearly forty of them! And he had invested in his own stallion, with the rather majestic name Dalton van Doornenburg, a dapper little chestnut with long, thick flaxen mane and tail. This little stallion was very popular with other Shetland pony breeders and made 85 guilders per covering, which was a very helpful addition to the baker's income.

DALTON, THE SHETLAND STALLION EARNING
85 GUILDERS PER COVERING.

Not long after the oldest daughter, Thea, started riding lessons at a nearby riding school, she announced that she wanted to run her own riding school when she grew up. She was an extremely determined child and the baker and his wife knew that they had to take her seriously. Younger brother Jan, who was small for his age but with a tough and wiry build, also seemed to take a keen interest in riding.

Baker Oortveld had already had his eye on a small, rundown farm several miles from the bakery and waited patiently until he was able to buy it for tuppence. All the ponies were moved over to their new home and baker Oortveld scraped more pennies together so he could invest in a few ponies and horses suitable for riding lessons. An area was fenced off to serve as a very basic outdoor school - and so Thea was able to start giving riding lessons.

Now that they had made a greater investment in livestock, it was decided that Jan, being only just thirteen, would live on the farm in case there was a problem with one of the animals. Thea would deliver bread in the morning and after that go to the yard to work, bringing with her a cooked meal for Jan, who, after having biked back from school and finished the chores, would be on his own for the rest of the evening. He would reheat his food, eat it, make his homework and go to bed. He never dared to complain about his lonely existence because, despite being a mere child, that was how he was brought up and he understood that there was no other way to make the business work. The only time he slept in his old bedroom at home again was the night before his wedding; that was how it was done in those days.

The business grew steadily and baker Oortveld became interested in the Arabian horse. He had a Welsh pony mare from the famous Coed Coch Stud and decided to put her to the Arab stallion Saoud. It turned out to be a brilliant choice because all the offspring were great competition ponies and the baker started to make a bit of a name for himself because of it.

In the meantime, Jan, now a few years older, plenty strong but still slight of frame, had gotten himself some rides as a jockey over hurdles. He loved it and his admiration for the thoroughbred was established. This experience partly formed the foundation for the kind of instructor he became in his later life, because he learned to understand the very sensitive character of the thoroughbred at an early age. The thoroughbred, which had gradually been introduced to the Gelderland and Groningen horse in order to breed a finer and more elegant riding and driving horse, certainly had an effect on the temperament; one could bully a draught horse into submission but not a thoroughbred.

§

Jan, by now seventeen years old, brought on a young bay gelding that was quite plain to look at, too long in the back and a big head with a roman nose, but was bold and with a good jump. Soon they were competing together. When winter arrived and everything was frozen up, jumping competitions were held in indoor schools, which most times didn't measure more than 30 x 15 metres. At one such show in the small village of Brummen, Jan cleared 1 metre 90 with El Capone and knew he was sitting on a special horse. That year they won the National Championship show-jumping.

But what he had to endure to achieve something so very special! Jan did not have his own transport. For every show he had to hack to a nearby cross-roads at the most ungodly hours, often in the dark. It could be freezing or blowing a howling gale. He dared not be late because he would be left standing, so he would wait patiently, soaking wet or cold to the bones, horse by his side and saddle under his arm, for the local cattle lorry, cleaned out with fresh straw for the occasion, which would collect more horses and riders on the way. Riders would all have to fit in behind the last partition which was no more than a wooden gate. There was enormous comradery and jokes, and raucous laughter would occasionally surprise a lonely biker, being passed on his way to work. Coming back, the losers had to brave it and share the elated joy of the winners. When time came to unload it was often dark and the ride home with a tiny battery-powered light stuck in the riding boot was tedious to say the least. And once at the farm there might still be some work waiting to be done. He would still have to heat his pot of food left by Thea before he could finally sit down, nearly too tired to eat.

It was even worse when shows lasted several days, such as the show at Boekelo. Jan brought a sleeping bag so he could make himself a bed on some bales of straw next to the stable where his horse was bedded down.

When the small, grey, Citroen two-horse van was acquired, which in its previous life had been a police van, competition life became much easier. It eventually was replaced with a second-hand red and white Bedford lorry, proudly showing the name of their riding school painted on the door, 'MANEGE DE LIEMERS'

JAN OORTVELD RIDING OUT FROM RIDING SCHOOL
'DE LIEMERS' WITH A GROUP OF CLIENTS.

When his sister Thea, by now very capable with her carriage horses, was on her way to a driving competition in Cherbourg, she found out that the Bedford, with a trailer for the carriage attached, found the hills a challenge, but, however slow, it never let her down and always would rumble on to the top, with Thea giving a sigh of relief.

This was during the time that the riding school changed premises in order for baker Oortveld to make yet another investment: an indoor arena! It was positioned in a stunning area, on the edge of Montferland, a gently sloping and pretty piece of countryside near the German border. The business took off big time with - other than the horses owned by the school and used for lessons - forty-odd stables gradually being filled with livery horses as well, a necessity since the overheads were now substantial, to say the least.

During the years while Jan was getting his qualifications, he was an intern at the equestrian college in Deurne for three months of the year; the rest of the time he worked at home. By the time Jan would be fully qualified, the business would then be able to upgrade to a recognized riding school, able to accept and train working pupils for Deurne. It became the most important training and competition establishment serving a large area.

§

They kept the Bedford lorry for many years and every now and then Thea would drive off and come back with a few horses in the back that she had bought on the way. She would just drive around and scan the fields and when something caught her eye she would drive up to the nearest farm in the hope she would find the owner somewhere. No farmer was ever able to pull the wool over her eyes because Thea did not like spending money; either it went cheap or not at all.

They did not always know an awful lot about the past of these horses. For example, one day Thea came back with a roan mare and a grey gelding. The roan mare arrived looking very poor and wormy with a prickly, dull coat and the only way to explain the big, white-haired scar all over her rear end was that she probably had been left in a field for the winter with a jute cattle rug fastened with binder twine that had ended up under her belly. She turned out to be one of the most willing and kind horses the riding school ever had, patient with the beginners and, at the same time, a keen and tidy jumper for the more experienced customers. The grey gelding on that same load turned out to be a cheerful animal, a real character, who loved humans and had been taught all kinds of tricks. On voice command he would step back or forward or halt when completely free and untethered. He was a very good mover and jumper, nearly too good for the riding school but very useful for the working pupils.

§

One wing at the Deurne complex, was designated to the Trakehners owned by Mr. van Doorn from the DAF factory who donated the land for this new equestrian college, which had opened its doors in 1969. Jan may have been national show-jump champion with El Capone, but he knew nothing about submission, self-carriage or riding a horse on the bit, and so, being a fresh arrival, he watched the famous George Theodorescu teach the two Van Doorn girls on their smart black horses which opened up a whole new world to him. Theodorescu had fled Romania in 1931 for political reasons and settled in Germany where he furthered his development as a dressage trainer. This great master was a much-liked and greatly admired horseman with the kindest of attitudes, able to win every horse over.

It didn't take Jan long to get settled in at Deurne and on Saturdays, when the morning chores were done and the rest of the day was his, he would take his stallion Kunstenaar around the international cross-country course on the premises, just for fun. Kunstenaar was one of several breeding products of the veterinary college 'De Uithof' in Utrecht. The university had horses for research that included mares with gynaecological problems and breeding was a necessary byproduct of their research. The chairman of the WPN, Mr. van der Mey was also a professor at the university, so Kunstenaar was bound to be a quality byproduct.

Kunstenaar was by Fresco out of a Wachtmeester mare. Fresco was a jumping machine owned by well-known breeder Henk van Tuyl, whose nickname was 'the Potato King' because that was how he began his business, which in the end grew into an international vegetable export business. Henk van Tuyl was a religious man and for his German show-jump rider Gerd Meyer this could be disastrous if a show was on both the Saturday and the Sunday, with the jump-off on the latter. On Sundays life stopped for Henk van Tuyl; on that day it was only the church that mattered.

When Kunstenaar was not used in Deurne he was standing at the riding school and he was not the only stallion who lived at 'De Liemers' at the time. The stallion Nooitgedacht was temporarily leased to 'De Liemers' by owner Griemelink, who, at his stud in Borculo, owned other quality stallions such as Exilio. When Nooitgedacht had to do the performance test in order to be accepted as a sire things hadn't exactly gone according to plan. The great conversion within the breeding world had only just begun and even the most experienced trainers and judges had yet to come to terms with how the character of horses changed when thoroughbred and draught horse were put together. Unfortunately, just before the sensitive and high-spirited Nooitgedacht was going to be tested in the harness for the studbook he had a little cold. He never left his stable for an entire week and nobody really took into account that this might be more than the stallion could handle. His performance was such that he scored very low for his character and this made Jan furious because he knew it was wrong. He loved riding Nooitgedacht, whether schooling or hacking, the stallion was always kind and willing. Nooitgedacht knew the difference between his exercise bridle and the halter with the Chifney bit, used for when he was going to cover a mare. With his bridle he was quiet and well-behaved, but as soon as he saw the halter he knew what was coming and he changed into a ball of fire.

JAN OORTVELD AT THE STALLION SHOW WITH THE STALLION NOOITGEDACHT, WHOSE LINE STILL EXISTS.

§

Having finished all four years of training at Deurne successfully, Jan couldn't wait to get home. Just before he left Deurne, he had met up regularly with Gonnie and he was keen to see her again.

Jan's father, baker Oortveld, had gotten himself a pair of very nice driving mares. It was quite a coincidence that Gonnie's father not only had a bakery in the next town, but also loved horses and soon both baker fathers, both Gonnie's and Jan's, now a bit older and thus with a more spare time on their hands, were regularly harnessing these two stalwart chestnut mares for jollies around the countryside. Also, whenever the agricultural magazine offered an organized trip to one of the breeding shows in Germany, they were sure to sign up together and join a busload of other horse lovers and breeders. When Jan could find the time he would join them. The Trakehner show in Neumünster, the Holstein auctions, the stallion parade at Warendorf, with every outing the world opened up a little more to them.

In 1980 a temporary wooden floor was laid on the sand of the indoor school of riding school 'De Liemers' for a very special and festive occasion. For one night Jan moved back to his old bedroom in the family house that he had left when he was thirteen for his lonely existence at the farm- this in order to conform to an old custom. The next day he married Gonnie and it did not seem a long time before they were a happy family with two young daughters who both loved their ponies.

§

A few years ago, Jan decided to start anew and set up a small but very satisfying business for himself, fully supported by Gonnie, a training facility for aspiring event riders with Jan being the patient and experienced trainer, able to turn any tricky moment around with the cheeky sense of humour he has never lost. Some forty years ago, event riding was still very new to the Netherlands but Jan was already fully involved. And at the time of writing he's a very fit man at sixty-two and going strong with his mare Doortje!

7

ROELI BRIL

LITTLE ROELI WITH THE WORKHORSES IN THE FIELD.

ROELIE WAS FOUR YEARS OLD when his parents happened to run into Roeli's uncle in the street on the off chance, when going for a stroll in their hometown of Zutphen. Roeli's uncle took one look at the chirpy little child, who was trying for dear life to scramble out of his pram, and invited him and his parents up to the coal merchants yard in the middle of town, run by Roeli's uncle and grandfather, in order to meet the horses. From then on horses were all Roeli's tiny head could think of. When his uncle saw his beaming face, with the two chubby arms stretching out to the big trustworthy faces of the cart horses, resting after a hard day's work, he knew he had made a little friend and so it happened that this became Roeli's second home until eventually, as a grown man, he moved in and took over the business.

ROELI AS A TINY LAD IN THE DRIVER'S SEAT, WITH A RATHER LARGE PLASTER ON HIS KNEE, DURING THE CARNIVAL PARADE IN ZUTPHEN.

§

It was just after the Second World War and Roeli's dad worked for a shipping company where he managed the storage rooms, a job that did not give the family a lot of financial leeway, to say the least. His parents had no interest in horses whatsoever, so Roeli's uncle became a lifeline, because he offered Roeli the opportunity to develop himself as a horseman, a miniature horseman but nevertheless a horseman. Although his uncle and grandfather had the three or so workhorses, they really knew very little about them, other than that the horses needed food in order to work. That was how it was in the days when horses were just a general means of transport.

Eventually Roeli convinced his uncle to invest into a finer built horse, which was still able to pull the coal carts but also able to take Roeli to the riding club, something he craved for. This was not a straightforward matter because the nearest riding club was Gorssel and very upmarket, too, most of the members being big farmers. The whole business was to be a subject at the next club board meeting.

§

Roeli finished school at sixteen and soon got all the qualifications he needed in order to work full time for his uncle. His grandfather had only just retired and so the business needed Roeli. During that time the number of coal merchants in the area went from twenty-three to five or six because none of the others had successors. It was hard work. During the summer they shovelled the coal from the train carriages into bags and onto their own carts, then they shifted the bags to their storage area. Deliveries happened all year around because, for example, the owners of the smart townhouses in Zutphen did not want for those sooty men walking all the way up at least two sets of stairs to the attic, where their coal was stored, during the cold and wet autumn and winter months. Those deliveries took place during summer. By the time the coal merchants got to the last set of steps and into the boiling hot attic with virtually no ventilation, they could barely feel their legs anymore. Roeli was adamant: only one bag per man, and not two as many of the workers preferred. Although he himself would carry two, he knew from experience how quickly the legs of the young lads would give way after several of those trips and the mess it would make.

Not only did they deliver coal, they shifted all kinds of goods, bread for example, which filled the gaps when coal was slow. Or if there was a wedding or a funeral, the horses would be put to use and a little more money was made.

IF THE COAL WAS SLOW, A FUNERAL OR WEDDING WAS ALWAYS A GOOD WAY TO MAKE A FEW EXTRA PENNIES.

§

In the summer Roeli rode as much as he could, but when the dark evenings and frosty ground made it impossible to do so, he did the other thing he loved so very much, speed ice-skating. In those years the winters were still cold and the canals and the flooded land along the rivers were hard frozen for many weeks at the time. On the big pond in town, the very keen skaters would sweep the ice after it had snowed in order to keep a decent track going. In the early sixties the speed skate arena in the nearby town of Deventer was opened, which came in handy when winter was not so cold.

Skating kept him fit in order to pick up the horse training as soon as the ice had melted and the days grew longer again. Then Roeli on his bike, horse trotting along with him, would peddle along to the cattle market at the other end of town, which was the nearest space available were he could pursue the art of horsemanship.

One day they had a coal delivery for mister Joostink, a pleasant man with a huge beard, who asked Roeli whether he'd heard anything from the riding club. A year had gone by since Roeli had first asked but to no avail, he regretted to say. Mister Joostink did not like this much and obviously pulled his weight because, only one week later, Roeli received a letter telling him that he had been accepted as a member. He couldn't wait until the first club instruction came round and the days up to this momentous evening went tortuously slowly. When the day finally arrived, after having finished work, he saddled his horse and made his way to the outdoor school of the club, some seven or so miles from town, but somewhere along the way, because he wanted to arrive well-prepared, he decided to have a small lunging session in a little school he knew. Disaster struck: the lunge line broke as soon as Roeli let the horse go longer. Somehow he managed to get close enough to grab the horse's neck and hung on for dear life. The two neared the railway going faster and faster and Roeli got hit in the head by something, ending up unconscious along the track in the bushes.

Feeling very proud of his son's achievements, father Bril had decided to surprise his son and bike over to see him ride at this prestigious riding club. He could not believe his eyes when the riderless horse came cantering towards him although actually this was lucky because Roeli's dad, worried sick, immediately went looking for him. In fact, both horse and rider were very lucky because the horse came home safely and, after a very serious and daring operation to remove pieces of bone from inside his skull, Roeli also recovered fully and surprisingly quickly.

Several months later, Roeli was once more on his way to his first lesson. He introduced himself to the extremely well-respected instructor Manger Cats, a retired army officer, who told him to go to a corner of the field and start practicing riding straight lines. This went on for several weeks, Roeli would say hello, riding his straight lines on his own in the corner, and say goodbye when leaving again, wondering what the hell was going on. He never found out but, after several weeks, instructor Manger Cats decided Roeli had done plenty of straight lines and told him to join the group and, after a few months, Roeli was able to take part in the festivities organized for the Queen's' birthday in the town of Deventer, which involved a performance of the riding club.

§

Horses were not entirely ruling Roeli's life. He found the time to fall in love and it didn't take all that long before Roeli and his fiancée Toos got married. Toos understood Roeli's passion and was incredibly loyal and supportive. There was only one problem: in order to keep its customers happy, the coal merchant business decided to invest in a proper little lorry with the inevitable consequence that the horses were sold off, including Roeli's ride. Money was short and a horse for pleasure was not something they were able to afford.

Two proud men, Roeli on the left, with their new little lorry.

This problem was easily solved by a local farmer, who did a bit of dealing on the side. He had seen Roeli ride and would kindly loan him the odd horse. This soon became a daily trip, every evening after work had finished, Roeli would bike over to the farm some six or seven miles away where he would break and ride everything available, never leaving until the stables were tidied up after.

Roeli continued to love his lessons with Manger Cats, the man who initially treated him in such a curious way. Manger Cats gave the young and ambitious rider the foundation he needed for the future and it was Manger Cats who, in the latter part of the sixties, suggested that the riding club ask Roeli to become their instructor. By then Roeli was more than accepted by his fellow riders and thrived in the supportive atmosphere of the club environment. He was aware, though, that he lacked the qualifications as an instructor and followed all the necessary courses to complete his mission as a professional horseman and instructor.

§

In the meantime, Roeli and his forever supportive young wife Toos managed to save some pennies and they bought Olaf, a five year-old grey by a thoroughbred, something virtually unheard of and a new development in the breeding world at the time. Olaf cost 1,275 guilders, including a saddle and some left-over bales of hay. In order to make the training at home easier, Roeli brought in riversand and dumped it in the coal merchant yard which now doubled as a small training area, and this was where Roeli started giving private tuition, with Olaf looking at it all from over his stable door.

Roeli and Olaf bonded so very quickly that, within the year, they became Advanced dressage and grade-A show-jumping champions. This, despite the lack of shows because competitions were sparingly organized and not easy to get to. Very often it was the horse which was the transport, the tidy kit of the rider hidden under an old coat and breeches, that or the local cattle lorry which was cleaned up for the occasion.

Roeli and Olaf during an event. Roeli is wearing the unusual hat, specific for Riding Club 'Gorssel'.

Their success did not stop there. The very next year, Roeli and Olaf qualified for the Europeans in Austria after having won both the National Championship dressage and the Gelderland Championship grade-A show-jumping.

During the run up to the Europeans some of the team training took place far away in the south of the country, in the province of Limburg with trainer Wiel Hendrickx, which was of course impossible without transport. Roeli and Toos went into their savings once more in order to fork out for a trailer.

Roeli rang the bell at the front door of a GP near Amsterdam who had two trailers for sale and a horse that wouldn't load, and, to his surprise, he recognized the horse looking out of its stable. It was a horse that had been sold to the GP at a horse market not too long before and Roeli had been wandering around at the time and had talked to the seller. It had been a dreary wet day and the horse had been standing there feeling cold and miserable. When, towards the end of the market, the doctor asked if he could see the horse trot up, it was so pleased to be moving, its tail went up and it trotted, its coat shiny from the rain, as if its life depended upon it. The seller made more money than he could have possibly hoped for from the GP and now Roeli was able to by his much-wanted trailer from the man who could not load his horse in it.

The trailer was put to good use because not many horse owners had their own transportation. It earned its money back very quickly, bringing mares to Henk Nijhof, Johan Venderbosch and other studs or transporting horses which were sold to their new owners. Anything to support Roeli's sport.

§

After a couple of years Roeli was approached by some people from München in Germany, who offered 12,500 guilders for him, which was quite a profit and Roeli could not believe his luck. But Toos brought the deal to a grinding halt because she did not want Roeli and Olaf to part. She told Roeli quite clearly that she felt he would never have a horse like Olaf again, and she was right; it was Olaf who made Roeli Bril the competitor and instructor he was, who gave him a name and credibility - and Roeli was the first to admit it.

And although Olaf was quite famous by now, he still was put in front of the carriage for the odd wedding of an acquaintance. Where would you find a horse like that, ever again?

A Royal moment at the National Championships.

§

In 1972 the coal business finally went bust because natural gas had gradually taken over after enormous supplies of it were found in the north of the country. A tragedy really because it was not that long ago that they had invested in their little lorry and they were also only just virtually fully mechanized for shifting the coal from the train carriage onto their lorry. Roeli had already increased his hours of instruction in order to pay for his hobby and also, occasionally, he would buy and sell a young horse to make a bit of extra money - but he needed more than that to pay the bills.

A member of the riding club, an architect called Jan Brinkman, knew a piece of land where possibly an indoor school could be erected for the riding club. The club, however, felt it was too much out of their way, so Brinkman approached Roeli with a plan: Brinkman would buy and build it and Roeli and Toos would run it. Since the local tennis club next door had no canteen, Brinkman had the ingenious idea of creating a riding school with a joint canteen for the riders and the tennis players, with Toos running that part of the business and Roeli running the riding school.

This adventure lasted ten years. Toos and Roeli lived in a house built on the premises. They'd had their two boys by then and they had their hands full with not a spare minute left. If Roeli wasn't teaching, he was competing; if Toos wasn't pouring coffee or drinks, she was cleaning the canteen. Some years later, if Roeli was teaching or competing and their son Roelof, now in the pony club and competing as well, needed to go to a show, Toos might have to clean the canteen during the night in order to be ready in the morning to drive her son to his competition.

In 1984 the oldest daughter of Brinkman wanted to take over the business and Roeli and Toos had to pack their belongings. They moved to Enter where they became part of the business of breeder Henk Spekenbrink. Although son Roelof was excited to have the ride on two of Spekenbrink's stallions after school, Roeli kept driving back for lessons with his clients near Gorssel, being possibly a tad homesick as well. Toos joked and called herself his Bed-and-Breakfast because he was gone most days.

§

During the years Roeli was instructing the riding club of Gorssel-Zutphen, the club won the national club championship eleven times. Roeli himself competed five horses into Advanced dressage and grade-A show-jumping. It may have been common practice to compete in both dressage and show-jumping at the time, but to achieve the highest levels on several different horses, time and again, showed extraordinary horsemanship.

During this period, he also became the instructor for riding club Varsseveld, where Johan Venderbosch from stud 'De Radstake' was involved both as a rider and on the committee. Roeli was a young man. He was tough on himself and neither did he take any nonsense from anyone he worked with or instructed. This occasionally caused a few tears amongst some of the female club members which Johan would subsequently have to dry. However, as the years went on, Roeli matured into a most competent instructor who, standing patiently on the side of the arena and always, with his dry sense of humour, would come up with the key sentence which would help the rider to find another, better groove. His motivation and perseverance were infectious and caused many a rider to put in the necessary extra hours so as to show improvement during their next lesson. Varsseveld had this luxury for thirty-four years, for which service Roeli was made an Honourable Member.

He was never shy of taking on yet another challenge, from bondscoach for the Dutch eventing team to international eventing judge, for which he did a couple of courses in Saumur in France. He loved it all, always ready to spread his wings a little more. As the nephew of the local coal merchant he never ceased to marvel at all those fantastic opportunities, at being able to see so much of the world when travelling to the different international events: Punchestown twice, Badminton and Burghley and many more.

§

In 2001 the phone rang and a very nice lady asked Roeli to judge at an event somewhere in Canada. Roeli asked her several times to repeat her question because he could not believe his ears. Canada, in the middle of the Rocky Mountains! After the phone went down he quickly called his son Henk, who sometimes accompanied him on his trips. That September they excitedly boarded their plane to Calgary. They left a few days early so that on arrival they could pick up a rental car and do some sightseeing through the Rockies, but as they neared the area where the event was to take place they started to wonder whether they were in the right place at all - there was nothing other than a few houses very far apart! They found the house of one of the organizers and from there went to the neighbours who would be their hosts.

Next morning, watching the huge lake in front of the house steam heavily in the early sun, with temperatures climbing rapidly from well below zero to a pleasant autumnal level, Roeli and Henk were off. It was the first day of competition. Some of the competitors had travelled for well over two days to get there. The lorry park looked extremely colourful as it was filled with all kinds of vehicles, from small trailers to lorries in all sizes and shapes. Everything happened here at all levels - one, two and three-star - and all of this in the middle of nowhere, with one lady who was hired to do the catering and who produced the most delicious food. Judges were helping laying the tables and pouring the wine; simply everybody pitched in and the atmosphere was so very warm and friendly that Roeli and Henk were still full of it when they flew back, just in time for the Dutch international event in Boekelo, so very different with all its luxury at the 'autumn-fair' stands.

§

Roeli has passed on his knowledge to so many riders. Not the least to his son Roelof Bril who, together with his wife Heike, runs his own professional yard in Westendorp. Despite his lung problem and despite being not far from eighty years-old, Roeli has never been able to stay away from the riding area for very long and, at the time of writing, is still out there, on the side of the arena, sharing his expertise.

8

A VISIT TO THE NATIONAL STALLION SHOW 2016 IN DEN BOSCH

It was 7.30 in the morning when my close and lifetime friend Elze drove up in front of my sister's house in Zutphen to pick me up. After a heartfelt hug because we had not seen each other for a year, I shoved my weekend bag in the boot and we drove across the old bridge over the river IJssel, which was rising so fast after heavy rainfall in Germany, you could see the water swirling angrily in its attempt to flood the fields, steadily crawling up the dyke.

While the TomTom told us where to go, Elze drove and we chatted excitedly, trying to catch up on everything, from dogs being ill and mothers growing old to how the last dressage competition went and the boring and tedious slug on a smallholding through a very warm and wet winter.

In a little over an hour we reached our destination, the Brabanthallen, a huge complex in Den Bosch where the national KWPN stallion show had started a day earlier with the show-jumpers. Because Elze was only able to take two days off work, we had chosen the last day of the show-jump stallions and the first day of the dressage stallions. The time had long gone that all qualified stallions fitted into one day.

After buying a catalogue, which added serious weight to my bag, and a cappuccino from a coffee bar with at least ten choices of coffees, we found ourselves some decent seats; it was fairly early and not too busy yet. The serious and businesslike voice of the announcer through the speakers encouraged us to watch with concentration as we settled down. Each stallion went through the same procedure. First he showed off his paces within the smaller ring, the lunging whips, professionally used by the lads in their white shirts and trousers, sending the horse in the desired direction, proceeding onto the track with the three fences, the first two being uprights and the third one a spread. After having done that several times, and with the fences gradually going up in height, the stallion was put back on the lead and shown one more time by his handler, hopefully showing himself well in his best trot. When each section had finished, all stallions were walked back into the arena and the chairman of the judges' panel informed the public which stallions would proceed to the third-round viewing. In this decisive part of the KWPN stallion selection process, tension soared even higher for owners and handlers as they were waiting to re-enter the now cleared arena with their stallions in hand one more time, in order to show them individually in walk and trot. All the while the judges looked on, discussing and deciding whether each stallion would be given the chance to take part in the performance test or not. Also, there was the championship to qualify for.

 I made notes in order to see how close, or how far off, my own opinion was from the opinion of the judges. In the meantime greedily munching away on the endless supply of food Elze had brought, not only to keep the costs down but also so that we would not lose our good seats during the breaks.

 The generally quiet crowd during the selection process showed their appreciation very clearly when the stallion In Between from stud 'De Radstake' was trotted up in hand and stole the show with a splendid performance. I was quietly hoping he would make the championship, being loyal to Johan Venderbosch, to whom I spoke in 2015, when researching for this book. When the judges agreed with the public and made In Between champion, it was special to see the next generation, both Henriette and her brother André, proudly and with big smiles walk up in order to receive the big bouquet of orange flowers. Although I had not seen him, I knew Edward Bleekman had come over from the UK and I hoped he would be there watching and celebrating together with his old boss Johan Venderbosch.

JOHAN, HENRIETTE AND ANDRÉ WITH THEIR 2016 CHAMPION STALLION IN BETWEEN. INCIDENTALLY, HIS SIRE IS TOULON, WHO IS BY HEARTBREAKER. HEARTBREAKER BECOMING 2015 KWPN HORSE OF THE YEAR. SMALL WORLD AGAIN!

§

The evening show-jump classes again proved how the older generation had produced a new, competent generation of riders. Willem Greve, son of well known veterinarian Jan Greve who many years ago bought Voltaire together with Henk Nijhof Senior, rode and won with both Grandorado TN and his father Eldorado, the first in the five-year-old class and the latter in the 1.60 m class.

When the KWPN Horse of the Year 2015 was announced that evening, Henk Nijhof Senior watched Henk Nijhof Junior charge around the arena with 27 year-old Heartbreaker, who was behaving like a 3 year-old while the music and a standing ovation urged both of them to the verge of being out of control. Although I did slightly worry Heartbreaker would end up with a heart attack, I felt excited as I saw the pride of this family, fully deserving this great and honourable position; the result of several generations of solid dedication.

HEARTBREAKER ENJOYING THE SUNSHINE BACK HOME AFTER HIS EXUBERANT APPEARANCE AT THE STALLION SHOW 2016.

Late that evening, overwhelmed with information and by the spectacle, Elze and I drove to our hotel, which was fully booked and still lively with fellow show-goers having a last drink. We decided to call it a day and rolled into our bed in order to be up bright and early for the first day of the dressage stallions.

The next morning for breakfast, the atmosphere was that of one large family and small, friendly conversations flowed between the guests.

Back at the show, Elze and I settled into the same routine as the day before, however, this time we sat and chatted with a group of experienced breeders, all friends, a jovial atmosphere but also extremely informative. At lunchtime we were included in the sharing of a bottle of wine or two as the jokes became a tad livelier. I still managed to keep track and do my homework but this time I found it less easy to be close to the opinion of the judges. I soon realized that my humble taste was heeling towards a slightly more old-fashioned horse, possibly because I was not able to outgrow a desire to see the dual-purpose horse from the past. During one of the breaks I found myself chatting to some English breeders, seated in front of our gang. They felt the same and we were all slightly confused with the route the judges of the KWPN seemed to take, especially given the at-times overactive hock action that was of concern to most of us there.

Overhearing my conversation with the English breeders, my neighbour, an equine veterinarian, explained the gradual change that the stallion show had undergone during the years and this helped to clarify some of what I was seeing. When, some time before, I had spoken to Edward Bleekman, he had talked about the good old days when the stallion show was no more than a thorough selection process with just the breeders involved, no glamour and glitter, no loud music and no evening shows. How things had changed. Comparing Bleekman's conversation with what my friendly vet neighbour was telling me, made it all crystal clear: this was so much more than a national selection process. This had become a show for the entire international breeding world of the sport horse. After the show it would all settle down and the qualified stallions would go home in order to wait for the start of the performance test. That, my new vet friend told me, was really when the truth would prevail, because all stallions would have the same treatment and training at the equine centre at Ermelo.

Some 220 stallions took part at the show this year. Nearly 100 stallions qualified for the performance test. Last year's result told me that at least half of them would probably not pass that test. After that the stallions who were now accepted would still have to show their offspring several times during the years to come. It has to be a long and vigorously ruthless selection process, in order for the KWPN to not only have achieved, but also to maintain its prime position in the horse world.

For some years now, it has been possible for stallions to enter the studbook later in life, through their competition results, and, because of modern technology, the stallions are able to have an uninterrupted competition season. This is when many professional riders have a great chance to compete these stallions successfully and from which the breeders gratefully pick the fruits. At the time of writing, Willem Greve is riding some of Team Nijhof's stallions, Roelof Bril, trainer and competition rider and son of Roeli Bril, rides some of the stallions for 'De Radstake', yet another great example of the close relationship between several generations of riders and breeders that carries on to this very day.

§

Old rusty trailers have become smart lorries with large and luxurious living spaces, fancier than my own living room; TomTom's make sure we do not get lost; often the thermos flask is left home because fresh cappuccino from the coffee bar tastes so much better - the KWPN stallion show has grown into a show which attracts people from all over the world.

And that is so very much the strength of the Netherlands, which is such a little country that it has to look across its borders in order to succeed in the big, wide world. Which is why it took brave farmers such as Johan Venderbosch and Henk Nijhof to dare to venture out and find their stallions across the borders; and why coal merchant Roeli Bril went from strength to strength, moving from being a local trainer to bondscoach and international eventing judge; why Jan Oortveld, son of baker Oortveld, ventured away from the still fairly slow and stocky warmblood of the seventies and invested in a Selle Français in order have a faster time X-country.

And it is why I so very much wanted to go back home, to Gelderland, in order to find out what made them tick. The answer was simple: a huge drive and something in their veins that I recognized. We are back to where we began: the enormous desire to spend one's entire life with horses.

§

The drumroll sound of hundreds of wooden shoes, whether of farmers, coal merchants, bakers or any others with a great interest in the horse breeding, has been replaced by loud music, standing ovations and the clapping hands of some 25.000 visitors. Just as with everything else, evolution and modern times have put their stamp on the horse world and there is no point in trying to decide whether that's a good or a bad thing because it is unavoidable. However, in order to move forward we have to remember and value the knowledge available to us from the past, from the people who lived and worked with their horses, depended on their horsepower, literally, whether in front of the plow on the farm, delivering bread or pulling the coal cart.

AFTERWORD

THE VOICE RECORDER IS TURNED OFF and the only sound is the crackle of the woodfire in my work room. It surprises me strangely, as if I didn't see it coming, and it makes me sad to leave the people behind who have been talking to me for the last few months. Their stories brought me back to my youth and to a countryside and life which is ingrained in my soul. They also sent me on a research voyage because there was a lot to learn and major gaps in my knowledge.

It took a huge learning curve for me to be able to get these men to tell me the stories I hoped for. Henk Nijhof Sr. had to be lured back to the past time and again; he is obviously driven and thinks ahead all the time. Johan Venderbosch was technically very specific about explaining the time of the associations and after a long warm-up, to my great relief, he all of a sudden found the groove and it was easy. Jan and Gon Oortveld have been friends and we hadn't seen each other for a while, so the interview was interspersed with my own stories and awkward to dissect to say the least. Roeli's interview had to be postponed because of a stay in the hospital - his lungs were giving him problems - but when we finally got together, he sat down, started at the beginning and in the most natural way gave me a well-organized picture of his life, completely ignoring the fact that oxygen was in short supply. He was matter of fact, extremely efficient with no extras, just as he was and is as a trainer.

They all helped me to recreate their characters as well as I was able and to recreate an atmosphere that I felt was right for that time. In the hope I did not abuse their trust.

My choice of who to include is, of course, far from complete and entirely based on the trainers and studs who played a greater or smaller part in my youth and to whom and for which I am so very grateful. My apologies to all the great horsemen whom I have perforce left out; this was not meant to be a complete study but rather an impression, a snapshot, from a crucial era in the breeding of the Dutch Warmblood as a modern sport horse and of how my beloved Gelderland played a huge part in that and still very much does to this day.

Being a romantic at heart, one of the most touching moments during this project was on my first visit to the stud of Team Nijhof. When I asked whether I could have a look at the yard after we finished, Henk Nijhof Senior did not hesitate to give me complete freedom to wander around on my own since he had to leave to bring some sperm samples to a lab. I walked into the stable block with the stallions and suddenly, unprepared, I found myself standing eye to eye with the famous stallion Heartbreaker and I must admit, I found it humbling. I was pleased to be on my own because it was kind of intimate, the way we both stood staring at each other...

EXPLANATIONS AND TRANSLATIONS

Advocaatje	Creamy, sweet, alcoholic drink made of egg yolks.
Betuwe	Area in the middle of Holland where endless amounts of orchards form a huge fruit industry.
Cadre Noir	A corps of instructors at the French military academy 'ecole nationale d'equitation' at saumur in the western france, founded in 1828, also performing as an equestrian display team.
De Toekomst	The future
Hanzesteden	Name for the merchant towns along the river IJssel, stemming from the 14th to 16th century
Jonkie met suiker	Dutch gin with added sugar, poured in a tiny little glass with a little spoon for stirring.
Oom	Uncle
Opperstalmeester	Equerry
Pikeur	Head groom
Tante	Aunt
National Riding Club Championship	Each team had eight members which together would ride the quadrille test. Three members would have to do an individual dressage test and three members would have to compete in show-jumping. The combined scores were the deciding factor for the placing of the clubs.

SOURCES:

Stamboek Vereniging Het Groninger Paard
Landschapsbeheer Gelderland
Bokt.nl
Wikipedia
KWPN

www.ingramcontent.com/pod-product-compliance
Lightning Source LLC
Chambersburg PA
CBHW060330050426
42449CB00011B/2712

THE FARMER, THE COAL MERCHANT, THE BAKER...